Se\  ;

to

VICTORY

Restoring the Power of Biblical Praise

EBED
PUBLICATIONS
In love, serve one another

by

Daniel D. Rodes

EBED Publications is a division of
The McDougal Foundation, Inc.,
a Maryland nonprofit corporation dedicated
to spreading the Gospel of the Lord Jesus Christ
to as many people as possible in the shortest time possible.

Published by:

ƎBED Publications
P.O. Box 3595
Hagerstown, MD 21742-3595

ISBN 1-884369-71-5

Printed in the United States of America
For Worldwide Distribution

DEDICATION

I lovingly dedicate this book:

To my faithful and precious wife, ESTHER, whose endearing friendship has refreshed me over the years in a way that words could never express.

To our wonderful daughter, NAOMI, who has worked patiently with me, helping me solve the computer difficulties we encountered while I was writing this book.

I am grateful to both of them for their typing of the manuscript, their continuous encouragement and their untiring efforts to prepare this finished product for publishing.

To our faithful workers here at TRUTH, LIGHT & LIFE MINISTRIES. Without them, this worldwide ministry would not be possible.

ACKNOWLEDGMENTS

I want to express my gratitude to Brother HAROLD MC-DOUGAL for his help in the preparation of this manuscript.

I want to express my fondest appreciation to all those who have been a financial blessing to our ministry and for their prayers and encouragement as well.

Last, but not least, I want to express my deepest appreciation and gratitude to our church family at TRUTH, LIGHT & LIFE MISSION of Penn Laird, Virginia, who have been a great encouragement in making these Seven Keys to victory a reality. These precious people put these keys into practice and refused to remain in the comfort zone of tradition. They have been a great blessing to me over the years, with their love and kindness and faithful support of our ministry, standing with me through blessing and adversity.

CONTENTS

WORSHIP SONGS
BY DANIEL D. RODES

INTRODUCTION

Have you ever wished there were real answers you could give to those you know who are hurting? Have you ever looked at someone who was in bondage to sin or to a past hurt, or who was walking in unforgiveness or bitterness and wished there were something more you could do? What about your own life? Have you longed for more freedom in your walk with God?

Well, there are things we can do to gain victory in our life in Christ. Some of them seem quite simple, really, yet they are not always easy to carry out. We cannot just go through a spiritual recipe, walking once through each step and expect to be free. The keys we will look at here require changes in our way of living.

How did I learn of these keys to victory? One day, after I had been in prayer and fasting for our church, the Lord showed me that many of His children are in bondage and need deliverance from the things that hold them. He began to reveal to me the keys that would release His people from their chains of bondage. I was to teach these things in our church and on our radio programs.

I think the reason these simple keys are overlooked is because many believers have had religious traditions forced upon them, and they can barely discern the difference between religious opinion and the Word of God. In fact, tradition is often one of the bondages that must be broken in our lives if we are to have all that God has prepared for us.

As I continued in prayer, the Lord showed me a vision of the end-time army of the Lord. This was no weak, self-conscious, bound-up group of misfits. It was a victorious army of warriors who were going throughout the land with such power and strength that the nations of the world were shaken by their influence.

The Lord spoke to me and said, "My people have been living in the past. They have been holding onto their unforgiveness, grudges, and hurts for years."

He showed me that we, as pastors, shepherds over the people, bear a degree of responsibility in this regard. Many church leaders no longer believe what the Bible teaches and have begun to exchange the truths of the Word for the traditions of men. This has opened the door for the devil to attack our people because the Word of God has become *"of none effect"* in their lives (Mark 7:13).

In that vision, the Lord revealed to me that there are seven things the Church must do in order to maintain her freedom and fulfill the commission He has assigned to her. Each of these keys is found in the Word of God, but the practice of them is certainly not found in many traditional churches.

When I began to search the Scriptures in this regard, I was at first rather disturbed by the fact that some of the teachings seemed to be recorded for the Old Testament saints rather than for our own day. I also saw that if I accepted what God was telling me, I would have to forsake many of my traditional thoughts and teachings. After a thorough study of the Scriptures, I realized that I had been wrong, and I became willing to lay aside the opinions of men in order to embrace the clear teachings of God's Word.

These *Seven Keys to Victory* have become such a blessing to my own life and ministry that I now desire to share them with others. My goal is to help bring all of God's children into the fullest measure of blessing and deliverance possible, through learning to worship God in the way He deserves to be worshiped.

Some of the things you read here may be familiar to you, while others, perhaps, may not ever be seen in your church. Or, you may have seen someone else doing these things without realizing what exactly they were doing. Each key has an importance all its own, and each is supported by the Scriptures.

Some of the seven keys were easy for me to embrace, while I felt that others had been so misused that I hesitated to teach on them. I quickly realized that no matter how a gift of God has been misused, He expects His children to continue to show forth the genuine gifts in the fullness of His Spirit.

In recent years God has been restoring praise and worship to His people everywhere and many have experienced the power that comes with learning to praise Him. Many have received marvelous breakthroughs as they embraced the wonderful plan of God for His children to praise Him *"in every thing"* (1 Thessalonians 5:18). Still, many have not yet experienced the victory they need. I have come to believe that the key to their deliverance lies in expressing praise and worship to the Lord through a combination of the ways He showed me. If you are still living in defeat, I want to encourage you; the Lord has victory for you! He has not forgotten you. He wants to draw you closer to Himself.

As I see the results of the seven keys being put to work in the lives of various believers, I can't help but marvel at how people are being set free. They are coming into freedom from their past lives of pain and selfishness, as they move into a place of complete dependence upon Almighty God. As they respond to this teaching, we have seen people come into a new freedom and joy in the Lord. This is no temporary victory, which many people enjoy for a few days after some special conference. This victory has a lasting effect within the hearts of those who embrace it. When people respond to the Lord in the matter of praise and worship, their hearts are softened. They become more receptive to hearing the Lord speak to them, and they respond to Him, beginning to correct the things in their lives that have long hindered them from receiving the fullness of God.

It took some time for our own church congregation to get into the full sway of all that the Lord was revealing to us. It was not easy to break old traditions. Now, however, after several years, these things are so much a part of our regular worship that we have come to expect the manifestation of the power of God in every service. Visitors have sometimes exclaimed that there was a cloud hanging over the front of the church while we were worshiping or during the preaching. A visiting pastor saw an angel standing beside me as I preached.

Because we have been practicing these things now for several years, we know that if they are followed in a decent and godly manner, they will work. I now invite you, through these pages, to share some of the things that have happened to us.

We must all recognize that it is time for us, as the people of God, to rise up and gain victory over our own problems so that we can work to turn our nation back to God. Multitudes of hopeless and helpless people, in cities and towns throughout the land, are heading for an endless eternity without Christ, unless we can reach out to them before it's too late. We must be in a position to win these people, for this is the work our Lord has entrusted to us. I firmly believe that putting into practice these seven keys will enable us to prepare for the task ahead.

God is looking for obedient children whom He can use. Let us be those who operate our churches His way and those who proclaim liberty among the people of God. We can begin by learning to obey Him in the *Seven Keys to Victory*.

Daniel D. Rodes
Mt. Crawford, Virginia

PART ONE:

HOW I LEARNED OF THESE KEYS

— 1 —

The Beginning

The message of this book is not drawn from the realm of theory; it has been born from the reality of what the Lord has done, both in my life and in the lives of those He has placed in the congregation I pastor. It is my hope that it will bear fruit in bringing life to you as well.

This message began to come to me back in the eighties when I was led of the Lord to teach on the book of Acts. My thoughts and, as a result, my teachings, were all focused on the wonderful personalities and events of the early Church. The healings, the miracles, the evangelism, the power ... It seemed that those early believers could see the Lord at work continually in their lives.

In the midst of my teaching that series, one of our deacons said to me, "Every time you talk about the people in the book of Acts, I feel about two inches high." I could understand his feelings because I felt exactly the same way. Even though I was teaching about the Spirit of the Lord moving and about the things He was doing through His Church in the first century, I had not yet known that power in my own life. Something was missing, but I didn't know exactly what it was or how to get it.

Although I was experiencing more victory in my life than ever before, I had a deep desire for more of God. I grew more hungry every day as I prayed for His power to rest on me. I felt helpless, trying to minister to the needs of the people. It seemed that no matter what I tried to do, I needed more of God in order to do it effectively.

One day I'd had about all I could take of wishing for the power of God. I fell on my face before the Lord and cried out to Him to give me His power. "Lord," I prayed, "I either want Your power in my life so that I can effectively preach Your Word and lead Your people, or I want to resign. I can no longer stand to be a powerless preacher." I continued this intense plea to God for several days.

A few days later, as I was kneeling before the Lord, I did something I had never done before; I raised my hands far above my head toward Him. "Lord," I prayed, "John the Baptist spoke of You, saying that

16

You would baptize Your children with fire and the Holy Ghost. This is a promise of Your Word, the Bible. Lord, I need that power, that baptism, if I am to accomplish the work You have called me to do.

"God, You know I have been taught that the baptism in the Holy Ghost passed away with the early Church; but I can find no such teaching in Your Word. You empowered Peter, Paul, John, and many others with this power. Please give it to me, too, because You have *'no respect of persons.'* Based on the promises of Your eternal, unchanging Word, I right now receive the baptism of the Holy Ghost."

Instantly the power of God came upon me, and I began to praise the Lord in a way I had never known before. His power upon me was so strong that I asked Him to withdraw it just a little, lest I die. From that day forth I have had a strong desire, a craving, to praise and worship the Lord. When I began to ask Him how to better praise and worship Him, He referred me to the book of Revelation. There I read:

> *And I beheld, and I heard the voice of many angels round about the throne and the beasts and the elders: and the number of them was ten thousand times ten thousand, and thousands of thousands; Saying with a loud voice, Worthy is the Lamb that was slain to receive power, and riches, and wisdom, and strength, and honour, and glory, and blessing. And every creature which is in*

heaven, and on the earth, and under the earth, and such as are in the sea, and all that are in them, heard I saying, Blessing, and honour, and glory, and power, be unto Him that sitteth upon the throne, and unto the Lamb for ever and ever. And the four beasts said, Amen. And the four and twenty elders fell down and worshipped Him that liveth for ever and ever. Revelation 5:11-14

One day, not long after that, I heard a poet reading a poem he had written for a heathen goddess. He was adoring her, depicting her as sitting on a golden chair in the heavenlies. He described her greatness, her magnificence, and her beauty. I had never heard anyone worship in that way, and it disturbed me. *If a heathen can worship a nonexistent goddess like that,* I thought to myself, *why can't we worship the true and living God in such a way?* That day I learned the beauty and power of words in worship and, when I tried it, I found that I could worship God in the same way, expressing to Him all that was in my heart. I marvel that God had to use a heathen poet to teach me how to worship!

Then one day the Lord said to me, "I want you to begin to teach My people to dance, march, and shout before Me. They will become more victorious if they will obey these teachings of the Bible."

At first I really didn't want to get involved and I resisted. But the Lord kept gently encouraging me to train our people in these things. Slowly, but surely, I began to see that this was all part of His plan for worship — even though it had been overlooked by many churches for years.

Tradition has such a stronghold on us that anything new arouses protest, and we were no different than others in this regard. But eventually we did begin to obey the Word, and the Lord began to increase our understanding of the power of praise.

When we started obeying what the Lord was telling us, we began to gain more and more victories. Visitors coming to our church would comment time and again on the freedom they had experienced in our worship services. The anointing we were experiencing during our times of praise was taking away our burdens and breaking the yokes from our necks, just as the Word of God had promised (see Isaiah 10:27). No wonder Paul said:

Now thanks be unto God, which always causeth us to triumph in Christ, and maketh manifest the savour of His knowledge by us in every place.
2 Corinthians 2:14

For some of us, the issue may not be what we have to learn as much as what we have to unlearn. We must somehow clear up the distorted communications between us and a Holy God. We must trample under our feet the doctrines and commandments of men and adjust our thinking to the mind of Christ. We have paid a heavy penalty for our ignorance and for mindlessly accepting others' interpretations of God's Holy Word.

It took some time, but our local church body strove to become obedient to what the Lord showed us. We laid aside some traditions, choosing not to worry about what others might think, and we began to enter into the realm of rejoicing.

Although rejoicing, in itself, is not one of the *Seven Keys to Victory*, it provides the context for each of the seven. Why sing, or dance, or praise, if that act does not spring from a heart of rejoicing in our God?

— 2 —

THE RING OF REJOICING

I rejoice at Thy word, as one that findeth great spoil.   Psalm 119:162

As the members of our local church began to look to the Word to see what God had to say about shouting, marching, dancing, and other expressions of worship, we began to rejoice. And is it any wonder? We were coming out of man's traditions and into the richness of God's Word. If there is anything worth rejoicing about, it is the Word of God, the Bible. What a loss it would be to us if we didn't have this marvelous Book! As we explored what was written there, we began to rejoice more and more. We found a freedom that had been robbed from us by

21

the traditions of men. Truly, *"every word"* of the Bible is for our use (Matthew 4:4). As we continued to look into the Word of God, we began to experience more unity in the body. Soon we were able to obey the scriptural admonition:

> *Rejoice with them that do rejoice, and weep with them that weep.* Romans 12:15

While our emphasis here is on rejoicing, there is also a time for weeping. We must not walk in denial of those things that cause us to grieve or mourn. And when we are weeping, it is a blessing to find others who are willing to comfort us and to share in our time of sorrow. We weep with those who lose a loved one, or with those who are in some other time of sorrow or tragedy. We mourn over the sin that separates us from the sense of the presence of the Lord. In this world, there is much to mourn. Our Heavenly Father wants us to care for one another and to love each other. He said:

> *That there should be no schism in the body; but that the members should have the same care one for another. And whether one member suffer, all the members suffer with it; or one member be honoured, all the members rejoice with it.*
> 1 Corinthians 12:25-26

The Ring of Rejoicing

Just as we mourn with those who mourn, there is also a time when we should rejoice with those who are rejoicing. Unfortunately, jealousy sometimes enters in, encouraging backbiting and bitterness. When this happens, we are to repent of these attitudes which can only cause division within the Body of Christ. When we can rejoice when others are promoted or have been blessed, and when we can praise the Lord for them, then we will become a blessing to the whole Body, and the Lord will reward us in His own way. When we are a joyful, praising people, we will not be so quick to grow envious of our fellow Christians. We will learn to share in their gifts and in their achievements and success.

Our lives are to be characterized by continuous rejoicing, so we must decide to praise the Lord all day, every day. My attitude is my choice. I can choose to rejoice or to complain. When we come before the Lord with a heart of gratitude and thanksgiving, we open the door of blessing, and we begin to know what it means to have the favor of the Lord upon us.

Why was God displeased with the children of Israel as they wandered in the wilderness? Was it not because of their continual murmuring and complaining? They were experts at finding things to complain about. Did they spend their time thanking God for His guidance, for the clothes that did not wear out, for His provision of food and water? No. They complained about their conditions, about the leader God had given them, and even about his wife. They complained about their food and their lack of water. Because of such chronic complaining, God gave them *"leanness of soul"* (Psalm 106:15).

Israel's complaining was a result of her unbelief, and it led to separation from God. The Lord solemnly warned the people of what would happen if they did not obey Him in the matter of praising Him:

> *Because thou servedst not the Lord thy God with joyfulness, and with gladness of heart, for the abundance of all things; Therefore shalt thou serve thine enemies which the Lord shall send against thee, in hunger, and in thirst, and in nakedness, and in want of all things: and he shall put a yoke of iron upon thy neck, until he have destroyed thee.*
>
> Deuteronomy 28:47-48

It is easy to look back at Israel and point our fingers at what those people did wrong. But have we learned from their mistakes so that we do not fall into the same trap?

"THIS IS THE DAY"

> *This is the day which the Lord hath made; we will rejoice and be glad in it.*   Psalm 118:24

This verse is often quoted and sung — so often,

in fact, that it can be hard to get beyond the "feel-good" message it has been assigned. But let's lay hold of the meaning of this promise. We must get a revelation of the sovereignty of God. The Lord has made this day. He has formed it, and He knows what it will bring. He has ordained this day, and nothing can come to us today that He has not allowed. As we come to understand that He has made this day, we know that He is able to take care of everything that may come our way — whether good or bad. That is why we can say every morning: *This is the day which the Lord hath made; we will rejoice and be glad in it!*

Happiness is often a matter of choice. When you make up your mind not to counsel with fear or to befriend doubt, you are on your way to a joyful Christian life. There will always be troubles in this life, but just as surely as there are troubles, there is One to whom we can run with our troubles. Expect the Lord to work *all things together for [your] good* — even your problems.

When you make a decision to rejoice in the Lord every day, your faith will begin to soar. No one enjoys troubles, but those who face them with trust and confidence in the Lord are headed for victory. Everything in life looks a little different when you are determined to praise and give thanks to Him — regardless of what happens.

Many people never fulfill their deepest potential

in ministry because of their habit of displaying a snappy, disagreeable attitude. Sometimes it may appear that the "victim" of such characteristics has a justifiable reason for such conduct, but, in reality, this conduct is by choice. One of the best cures for overcoming such a habit is to begin praising the Lord and thanking Him for His deliverance every time you sense that disagreeable spirit rising up within you.

God showed my wife Esther and me the value of a life of praise years ago. We were quite busy one summer, traveling and preaching, and, although we had planted a garden, we didn't have time to care for it properly. I had planted some sweet corn, but a little later than usual. We were hoping to freeze some of it for the winter, as well as enjoy some fresh corn on the cob late in summer. Unfortunately, we had an early frost that year, and all of our sweet corn turned brown. I was disappointed.

We could easily have complained about the time and effort we had already put into that crop, time and effort which were apparently wasted. We chose, instead, to rejoice in the Lord and thank Him for what we had been able to harvest rather than dwell on that part of the harvest which appeared lost. Several weeks later, when I was clearing the garden for the season, I went out to cut down the corn stalks. To my surprise, I found full ears of corn on every stalk! We had fresh corn on the cob that day for lunch and called some of our neighbors to help us harvest the rest. Esther and I were delighted and praised the Lord for that extra blessing and gift of food for our family. We hadn't realized that God had planned a miracle for us. Our God is an awesome God, and it is so rewarding to live a life of praise to Him!

We have so much to be thankful for that complaining should seem foolish to us all. May God help us to be a grateful people. When we live a joyful and happy life, we are putting ourselves in line for God's wonderful blessings.

"REJOICE EVERMORE"

Rejoice in the Lord alway: and again I say, Rejoice.   Philippians 4:4

Rejoice evermore.   1 Thessalonians 5:16

Someone may ask: "How can I rejoice in the midst of disaster or calamity?" I personally believe that you will not have nearly as many problems in life if your life-style is one of rejoicing. Praise and rejoicing can head off a lot of troubles that we otherwise might face. Since Esther and I made a conscious decision to live a joyful, happy life, we have had a lot less trouble to deal with. And because we are joyful, even the troubles we do have to face don't seem nearly as bad as they might. Our focus has shifted from the difficulty to the Lord, and we are looking to Him who is able to hold us and carry us through the most difficult of times. We are looking to see how He will work what seemed like a terrible thing to His glory and to our good.

We saw this at work one cold, windy January day, when all the electricity went off in our area of the country. Heavy snow had caused the electric lines to fall. Without electricity, we had no heat in our house, and we could feel the cold air forcing its way in through every crack.

Esther and I and Naomi, our daughter, stood in agreement and asked the Lord to keep our house warm. Although the electricity was off for more than seven hours, the temperature in the house never dropped below sixty-eight degrees. What a gracious God we serve! If we can always rejoice and refuse to complain, the Lord will be ready to perform great miracles for us under the most difficult of circumstances.

Rejoicing must become a way of life. This can only be accomplished when we make a firm decision that regardless of what a day may bring forth, *"[we] will rejoice and be glad in it."* What can we do on the days when bad things happen? Let us look at what Peter had to say:

> *Wherein ye greatly rejoice, though now for a season, if need be, ye are in heaviness through mani-*

fold temptations: That the trial of your faith, being much more precious than of gold that perisheth, though it be tried with fire, might be found unto praise and honour and glory at the appearing of Jesus Christ: Whom having not seen, ye love; in whom, though now ye see Him not, yet believing, ye rejoice with joy unspeakable and full of glory. 1 Peter 1:6-8

Peter reminds us that we can *"greatly rejoice"* even when we are undergoing the most difficult tests of life. When everything seems to be going wrong, it is time to start rejoicing, for after the fire has tried us, our faith will be found to be *"more precious than gold."*

Peter continued:

Beloved, think it not strange concerning the fiery trial which is to try you, as though some strange thing happened unto you: But rejoice, inasmuch as ye are partakers of Christ's sufferings; that, when His glory shall be revealed, ye may be glad also with exceeding joy. If ye be reproached for the name of Christ, happy are ye; for the spirit of glory and of God resteth upon you: on their part He is evil spoken of, but on your part He is glorified. 1 Peter 4:12-14

Is it really possible to *rejoice* when we go through

fiery trials? Is it really possible to *be glad* when people speak evil against us? To the carnal mind, this makes no sense at all. This is one area in which our minds must be renewed if we are to walk in spiritual understanding.

God wants us to rejoice. Our focus is not to be upon life's difficulties, but upon His work in our lives. Happy, joyful people walk in victory every day, for God is with them. Even in times of great trouble they can see the hand of God at work.

On another such occasion our family reaped the benefit of rejoicing in God during difficult times. One cold winter's day, when we were living in the mountains of West Virginia, our house caught on fire. About fifteen inches of snow lay on the ground, and the temperature was in the teens, making it difficult for the firemen who arrived. They had great difficulty keeping their water hoses from freezing. As large billows of smoke ascended into the cloudless sky and our home was being destroyed before our eyes, Esther and I took each other by the hand.

"Daniel," she asked me, "What are we going to do?"

It would have been very easy in that moment to give in to fear and worry or to rage over what was happening to our home, but that was not the response the Lord wanted. That was not the way He had trained me to think. So I smiled at her and an-

swered, "We are going to praise the Lord and rejoice that we all got out safely."

Esther agreed with me, and so we stood there rejoicing. The fire marshal came and told us that we
must be in a state of shock to act as we were. He
suggested that we get to a doctor and request medical attention. We just laughed. "Sir," we answered,
"we have a mansion in Heaven that cannot burn
down. We have far more to live for than this earthly
house!"

When some of our friends came by to sympathize
with us over our loss, even they thought we were
behaving strangely. We explained to them that we
had no reason to weep, and that we preferred to rejoice. We were not pretending to be happy. It was
sincerely not an act. God's comfort was ours as we
rejoiced in Him and in His decisions for our lives.
When you make a decision to live a life of rejoicing,
you will find that the Christian life is the most rewarding life there is.

It is one thing to rejoice when things go wrong,
or when bad things happen to us that could happen
to anyone, but what about those times when evil
befalls us because we are doing what is right? It
helps to look at the attitude of the early believers
during such times:

> *And when they had called the apostles, and beaten
> them, they commanded that they should not speak*

> *in the name of Jesus, and let them go. And they*
> *departed from the presence of the council, rejoic-*
> *ing that they were counted worthy to suffer shame*
> *for His name.*   Acts 5:40-41

Can you imagine people rejoicing because they were worthy to be beaten for the Lord's sake? Yet the disciples literally rejoiced because the Lord considered them to be faithful enough to be beaten for Him. Human flesh has a tendency to shrink from suffering, but there is something about suffering for the Lord's sake that adds value to a life. It is not God's will for us to be sad and gloomy, even in the midst of suffering. He desires that we be full of joy.

If we could only understand that truth, what a difference it would make in our everyday lives! If God hadn't wanted us to be happy and joyful always, Christ would not have said:

> *These things have I spoken unto you, that My joy*
> *might remain in you, and that your joy might be*
> *full.*   John 15:11

There can be no doubt. The Lord wants us to be continually filled with His presence and joy.

The Apostle Paul learned the secret of rejoicing. He learned that joy does not flow from one's outward circumstances, but rather from the Lord God Himself. Joy is one of the fruits of the Holy Spirit and is found in people who are communing with God and producing the fruit of righteousness. Paul wrote:

Great is my boldness of speech toward you, great is my glorying of you: I am filled with comfort, I am exceeding joyful in all our tribulation.
2 Corinthians 7:4

Only a victorious, overcoming Christian could say something like that. That anyone could be joyful in tribulation doesn't make sense to the natural mind. James verified God's will in this regard:

My brethren, count it all joy when ye fall into divers temptations. James 1:2

"How could he write such a thing?" some might ask. "Didn't he understand that we all have bad days when our hearts are filled with sorrow?" Our present generation seems to wallow in victimhood and seek affirmation of its woes. Apparently James didn't understand that type of thinking.

And I don't understand it either. Personally, I believe that we Christians should forget most of the self-help books available to us today and the tapes that are supposed to help us get over all the hurts of our wounded spirits and build our self-esteem. If we would just dig into the Bible and find all the promises that relate to victory and rejoicing, we would know more joy and success in our Christian lives.

Many pastors teach that life is full of sorrow and disappointment and cannot seem to get any other perspective. Their minds are set on the negative aspects of life. How can they impart to us what they don't have themselves?

I have been harshly criticized by some for displaying a joyful spirit when I preach at funerals. Rather than dwelling on loss, I choose to preach about Heaven and the rewards that await those who choose to go there. One pastor said to me, "At a funeral we are supposed to *'weep with those who weep.'* " What he didn't know was that the family involved in that funeral had expressed their appreciation to me for giving them encouraging words rather than adding to their grief.

Religion has often portrayed life in less than realistic terms. While it is true that we must all sooner or later leave this world, we don't have to be like those who have no hope. For the believer, physical death is just a home-going. Yes, we do miss those who have gone on before. That is only natural. But we should also be happy for them that they preceded us to the presence of the heavenly Father.

Some people carry a spirit of grief around for years. I have ministered to people in various parts of the world who were still grief-stricken many years after a loved one had died, and when I prayed for them, they got deliverance. One pastor was surprised. He said to me, "I never realized that people could be delivered from the spirit of grief. I thought the Church was always to sympathize with those that mourn, but I have seen the results of deliverance. I have seen a remarkable change in the people. Some of them spent most of their time listening to programs that were supposed to help them; but these programs were actually making them worse. Now my people are rejoicing and praising the Lord. Instead of a life of defeat, they are now living a life of victory." Praise God! We can rejoice, even in the midst of troubles.

Paul and Silas knew about trouble. They knew about suffering for the Lord's sake. They were thrown into prison at Philippi for preaching the Lord Jesus Christ, but they didn't sit around weeping and pitying themselves. Instead, they burst forth with singing and praise, and their praise moved the hand of God. He sent an earthquake that shook open the doors and set the prisoners free.

The Philippian jailer and his family were saved as a result of what they witnessed that night in the prison. But what would have happened if Paul and Silas had been complaining about their lot instead of rejoicing and praising the Lord? Would the same thing have happened? Surely not! When we make rejoicing in the Lord a way of life, He is ready to work on our behalf.

When we face some sort of trouble, our heads may

say to us, "This is not the time to rejoice. How can you give thanks to God when you are in such a mess?" Paul explained this barrier of the natural mind:

> *But the natural man receiveth not the things of the Spirit of God: for they are foolishness unto him: neither can he know them, because they are spiritually discerned.*   1 Corinthians 2:14

It never makes sense to the carnal mind to do what the Lord tells us to do. Our minds need to be renewed in spiritual understanding:

> *Because the carnal mind is enmity against God: for it is not subject to the law of God, neither indeed can be.*   Romans 8:7

Only when we become spiritually minded do we begin to understand the things of the Spirit, and one of the most important keys to becoming spiritually minded is to learn to praise and worship the Lord.

Paul and Silas did not decide to praise the Lord because they were in trouble and hoped for a way of escape. Praise was a way of life for them. When we make praise and worship a life-style, it becomes just as natural to rejoice in difficult circumstances as it is to eat, sleep, or get up and go to work. A life of praise is not based upon circumstances. It is a matter of choice.

"YET I WILL REJOICE"

Although the fig tree shall not blossom, neither shall fruit be in the vines; the labour of the olive shall fail, and the fields shall yield no meat; the flock shall be cut off from the fold, and there shall be no herd in the stalls: Yet I will rejoice in the Lord, I will joy in the God of my salvation. The Lord God is my strength, and He will make my feet like hinds' feet, and He will make me to walk upon mine high places. Habakkuk 3:17-19

Talk about a bad day! Habakkuk must have felt as though everything were going wrong for him. His fig tree had quit producing. His vines were barren. His olive tree wouldn't produce. His fields were fruitless. His flocks had all died, and his cattle stalls were empty. This man had trouble! In the natural, he had every reason to complain, but he said, *"Yet I will rejoice in the Lord, I will joy in the God of my salvation."* Habakkuk chose to praise the Lord in the midst of his problems.

How could anyone give thanks in such circumstances? Wouldn't it be more sensible to cry and to beg others to pray for you? Habakkuk was faced with a decision about how he would respond to the existing circumstances, and the decision he made shows us that he lived a life of praise. He refused to be pulled down by his circumstances. He knew that God was bigger than circumstances, and he boldly declared, *"He will make my feet like hinds' feet, and He will make me to walk upon mine high places."* Talk about optimistic! This fellow was not about to give up on life just because some trees had failed and some animals had died. Isn't that a wonderful way to respond to trouble?

The difference between Habakkuk's attitude and that of a complainer is that Habakkuk had made a decision to rejoice in the Lord — regardless of the circumstances. Most of us rarely have a day as bad as Habakkuk described, yet his story had a victorious ending. He was able to walk in victory because he refused to complain and, instead, fixed his eyes upon his Redeemer.

There is power in praise! Even if you seem to have lost everything in life, you can shout the victory — if you still have the Lord. Hallelujah!

ENCOURAGEMENT IN THE LORD

David is another biblical example of one who could look to the Lord rather than to his troubles. He and his men had been living with the Philistines as they hid from King Saul. They had actually gone forth at one point with the Philistines to fight Saul, but they were spared from having to do so because the Philistines feared that David's men would turn against them in the battle. So they were able to return home to Ziklag.

When they got home, they met a horrifying sight. The Amalekites had overthrown their city and burned it down, taking captive all who had been left behind when the men went to battle. Their families and possessions were all lost. David and the rest of his hardened soldiers wept until they could weep no more.

Some of the men began to grumble. Why should they continue to follow David? Here they were, living like outcasts among the Philistines, shunned even by their own army. They would not be able to easily return to their own nation. And what had their loyalty to David gotten them besides exile and the loss of their families? As they spoke thus, their anger burned hotter and hotter, and they got so riled up that they were ready to stone David.

David, too, had lost his family; it appeared that he had lost his followers; and now he was about to lose his life. What was David's response in that moment?

And David was greatly distressed; for the people spake of stoning him, because the soul of all the people was grieved, every man for his sons and

> *for his daughters: but David encouraged himself*
> *in the Lord his God.* 1 Samuel 30:6

David was a spiritual giant who had learned to spend much time in praising and worshiping the Lord. Consequently, he was not disturbed by the presence of giants or other enemies. God gave him wisdom to take control of his circumstances.

His own loss was great, and he understood the weeping of the other men, but he knew that weeping would get them nowhere. So he *"encouraged himself in the Lord his God."* After David had taken that attitude, nothing could stop him or his men. They pursued the enemy and overtook them, totally destroyed them and recovered their lost families, as well as their livestock and their other stolen possessions.

When we choose to abide in a place of praise, worship and thankfulness, we are strengthened during times of trouble. Our eyes are not upon our problems, but upon our God who is able to deliver us out of them all.

THE RING OF REJOICING

So what is the ring of rejoicing? It is the ring from which hang the seven keys to victory. Just as a key ring holds keys together, so does rejoicing hold together the seven keys we will be looking at now.

The Ring of Rejoicing

Each of the keys we will discuss flows from a heart of rejoicing. The heart that rejoices will find it much easier to give creative expression to praise and worship to the Lord. An attitude of rejoicing is the root from which the rest flows.

Let us now begin our journey, through the *Seven Keys to Victory*!

PART TWO:

THE SEVEN KEYS

— 3 —

THE FIRST KEY: PRAISE

The first key to victory in the Christian life is praise. Our lives are to be those of praise unto the Lord, for He alone is worthy to be praised. We want to look at a few expressions or forms of praise, as well as the reasons for and benefits of praising our God. David sang:

> *Delight thyself also in the Lord; and He shall give thee the desires of thine heart. Commit thy way unto the Lord; trust also in Him; and He shall bring it to pass.* Psalm 37:4-5

The word *"delight"* in this passage has to do with getting sport out of what you are doing, enjoying it. *"Delight [yourself] in the Lord"* then means enjoy serving Him. Enjoy doing the things He asks you to do. When you do that, you have the promise of receiving *"the desires of [your] heart."* The Lord will bring your desires to pass. Isn't that a wonderful thought?

How many times in life we have missed something the Lord wanted to give us because instead of rejoicing and delighting ourselves in Him when troubles came, we began to lose the vision of what we really desired in the first place. If the Lord didn't want to give us the desires of our hearts, why would He have proclaimed this promise so clearly in His Word?

Many people have missed their greatest blessings because of impatience. If they don't receive something right away, they conclude that it was not God's will for them in the first place. Such thinking has led many Christians into a state of confusion. This has happened in my own life at times. I have believed that God wanted to do something with me; but, because it didn't happen right away, I concluded that I had been wrong and the Lord didn't want me to do it after all. Later, the very thing I had been ready to give up on started to come to pass in my life.

I am certain that this has been the experience of many others as well. I don't suppose there is a man or woman alive who could boast that he or she has never become discouraged at any time and wondered if God would do what He has promised.

The First Key: Praise

The longer I have been working toward a life of continuous praise and worship, the more I see the necessity of standing on the promises of God until all of His promises come to pass in my life. As believers, we need to be like Abraham:

> *He staggered not at the promise of God through unbelief; but was strong in faith, giving glory to God; And being fully persuaded that, what He had promised, He was able also to perform. And therefore it was imputed to him for righteousness.*
> Romans 4:20-22

Abraham didn't even consider the possibility that God might fail to keep His promise.

When you are in a time of testing, don't consider the possibility of failure. Don't for a moment believe the lie that a promise of God will not come. Only consider Him who makes all things come to pass after the counsel of His own will. And know that His will, purpose, and desire is that His children live full lives of joy, happiness, service, and blessing.

Why Blessings Fail

One reason some people don't receive from the Lord is that they are discouraged and perplexed, not knowing whether the Lord will bless them, not even knowing if He wants to do so. Such people may say, "The Lord may or may not give us what we desire. After all, God never promised to give us our wants, but only our needs." Yet the Scriptures plainly tell us that our heavenly Father wants to give us the desires of our heart. If we commit our way unto Him, God has promised that He will *"bring it to pass."* I like that promise. Don't you? Jesus said *"[you] shall have them"*:

> *Therefore I say unto you, What things soever ye desire, when ye pray, believe that ye receive them, and ye shall have them.*   Mark 11:24

There are conditions to this promise: praying and believing. In other words, if your ways are God's ways, if you are delighting yourself in Him, if you are making a firm and unchanging decision to live a life full of the Spirit and the joy of the Lord every day, you qualify for the promise. God will give you the things you ask Him for.

If you find it difficult to praise the Lord, then ask Him to help you. He said:

> *I am the Lord thy God, which brought thee out of the land of Egypt: open thy mouth wide, and I will fill it.*   Psalm 81:10

The great I Am has said that He would fill your

mouth, and He will do it. He will place praise in your mouth, that your lips may be those that please Him.

Few things we do in life can be as rewarding as praise. When you praise the Lord, you forget yourself and your problems. You forget your trials and temptations. You forget about demonic attacks. Praise allows us to truly focus our attention and energy upon our Lord. Praise Him for lifting your burdens and continue, day by day, until you gain the victory.

CONTINUOUS PRAISE

I will bless the Lord at all times: His praise shall continually be in my mouth. Psalm 34:1

By Him therefore let us offer the sacrifice of praise to God continually, that is, the fruit of our lips giving thanks to His name. Hebrews 13:15

Many believers have gotten the idea that the word *"sacrifice"* in relation to praise means that we are to praise the Lord when we don't feel like it. Of course we ought to praise the Lord whether we feel like it or not, but the word *"sacrifice"* here has to do with giving an offering to the Lord as a gift, something given with thanksgiving. When the children of Israel sacrificed to the Lord, they gave an offering with rejoicing. We need to understand that *"the sacrifice of praise"* means giving to the Lord that which is due His Name. We are not to try to make excuses for ourselves. We must get to the place where we spontaneously praise the Lord because He is worthy, rather than praising Him because we are told to do so.

How often and for how long should we praise our Lord? According to these verses, God wants us to praise Him continually. That means all day, every day, both day and night.

The Word of God also instructs us to *"Rejoice evermore. Pray without ceasing"* (1 Thessalonians 5:16-17). Some people seem to think that this is an impossible thing to do. Quite simply the phrases *"Rejoice evermore"* and *"Pray without ceasing"* mean "Don't stop praying and don't stop praising." The joy some believers experience lasts about as long as a firecracker in the hands of a twelve-year-old boy, but the Lord wants us to make praise a way of life. We're not just to practice this lifestyle for a few days or weeks, but there is to be continuous praise coming forth from our hearts. This doesn't mean we have to go around saying, "Praise the Lord" all the time. The Lord wants us to have hearts of praise, however, and praisers (those whose hearts are filled with praise) often express their praise to the Lord.

If praise becomes a legalistic form, it loses its value, just like anything else the Lord asks of us.

The First Key: Praise

We must make a decision to be praisers. We must choose to praise our God continually. When praise is in your heart, it will come out of your mouth. What is in your heart will flow forth from you like a river.

AN ATMOSPHERE OF PRAISE

God is greatly to be feared in the assembly of the saints, and to be had in reverence of all them that are about Him. Psalm 89:7

We should be careful to consciously create an atmosphere of praise and worship in our homes, churches, and Christian schools. Such an atmosphere causes an awesome reverence toward a holy, mighty, and sovereign God.

Anytime we discontinue our praise of God as a way of life, we open the door to complaining, murmuring, and strife. A home should be a place where we *love* to be rather than a place where we *have* to be. Yet some homes are so full of strife that no one enjoys being there. Praise can change that. As you begin to praise the Lord, it changes the very atmosphere of your home. It might not be easy at first, for continual praise requires a death to self, as you cease looking at your problems and at yourself and begin to look more and more toward the One who is worthy of all praise.

It might take a while before you notice any change in your home, for Satan would love to hinder you in any way he can. But don't give up on your life of praise to God. The very day that you throw up your hands in despair may be your day of deliverance.

THE GARMENT OF PRAISE

To appoint unto them that mourn in Zion, to give unto them beauty for ashes, the oil of joy for mourning, the garment of praise for the spirit of heaviness; that they might be called trees of righteousness, the planting of the Lord, that He might be glorified. Isaiah 61:3

People who have a spirit of heaviness often vent their frustration on their friends and family. They may release their feelings through tears, anger, or harmful words. Yet frustration (with its various expressions) is not the answer. Praise is! We must replace *"the spirit of heaviness"* with *"the oil of joy."* If you want to put on some exciting "makeup," something that will truly increase your beauty, this oil will do more for you than any other cosmetic.

We are even to wear new clothes. We are to put on *"the garment of praise."* So toss aside that old cloak of complaining and put on something beautiful and worthwhile — the praise garment.

Rejoicing and gladness bring out the true beauty

of a person. A pure, clean, joyful Christian has an expression on his or her face that shows forth the innermost being. When we wear *"the spirit of heaviness,"* we can cause others to carry that same heaviness. But the spirit of praise is contagious, too! The Lord expects us not only to put on the garment of praise, but to keep wearing it.

A CHEERFUL COUNTENANCE

A merry heart maketh a cheerful countenance: but by sorrow of the heart the spirit is broken. All the days of the afflicted are evil: but he that is of a merry heart hath a continual feast.
Proverbs 15:13 and 15

We all like to be around people who have a cheerful countenance and, undoubtedly the Lord does, too. Paul wrote that *"God loveth a cheerful giver"* (2 Corinthians 9:7). I believe that if He loves a cheerful giver, He must also enjoy a cheerful live-er. What a continuous feast cheerful people have! Broken spirits are healed. Evil days of affliction no longer have control over the cheerful Christian. Praise God, there is a way out of our troubles:

He shall call upon Me, and I will answer him: I will be with him in trouble; I will deliver him, and honour him.
Psalm 91:15

53

As long as we live in this world we will have plenty of opportunities to grumble and complain; but when we make praising the Lord a way of life we can be joyful, even when we are facing trials and tests.

AUDIBLE PRAISE

Some people tell me that they cannot praise the Lord with an audible voice, so they just praise Him in their hearts. I don't question the fact that a person can worship the Lord in his heart, but I also believe that if one enters into the true spirit of worship, he will find it difficult *not* to express himself to his heavenly Father audibly. When you have a heart full of praise, you will want to express your deep emotions toward your great and wonderful Father.

When two people are in love, they must express that love or their relationship won't last very long. Couples in love often seem overly expressive to their friends.

Some people express a problem in not knowing what to say to God, but you don't need to be an intellectual or a well-known preacher or musician to give acceptable praise to Him. You need only have a pure heart, filled with love for your Redeemer.

If you are troubled by not knowing what to say, you might want to develop a biblical vocabulary, speaking forth the same words that the Bible uses. As he wrote the Psalms, David touched upon many experiences and emotions which we share. There are many other passages throughout the Bible that contain words and phrases of praise. You can use these to train your mouth to praise God's name.

Knowing some of the biblical names for God can help to broaden your faith. Learn to use His names as you praise Him.

Start praising God at the point of your need. If you are in trouble, He is your Strength. If you lack something, He is your Provider. If you have sinned, He is your Redeemer. He is all that you need.

Loud Praise

Making a joyful or loud noise in praise is usually associated with loud musical instruments, although it may be associated with shouting (which we will discuss later) or even with loud praying or reading of the Scriptures. This may be a means of building one's faith or of engaging in spiritual warfare. Loud praise may be a declaratory or extolling praise, one that declares God's glory and grace and greatness. It may not be necessarily directed to the Lord Himself, but to His people, as in Psalm 150:

Praise ye the Lord. Praise God in His sanctuary: praise Him in the firmament of His power. Praise

Him for His mighty acts: praise Him according to His excellent greatness. Praise Him with the sound of the trumpet: praise Him with the psaltery and harp. Praise Him with the timbrel and dance: praise Him with stringed instruments and organs. Praise Him upon the loud cymbals: praise Him upon the high sounding cymbals. Let every thing that hath breath praise the Lord. Praise ye the Lord.

Psalm 150:1-6

When we loudly praise the Lord, we disturb and often defeat the works of the devil. Loud praise is very important when we are pulling down strongholds. Sometimes it is the only possible response to the mighty things God is doing in our midst.

There are those who would strongly disapprove of such praise, considering it to be disturbing. Such people would likely remind us in a religious monotone, *"The Lord is in His holy temple: let all the earth keep silence before Him"* (Habakkuk 2:20). How will those people enjoy Heaven where *"ten thousand times ten thousand"* will shout with a loud noise?

MOTIVES IN PRAISE

While loud music and praise have their place, we do need to be cautious about their use. Many people are attracted to this kind of praise just because it's so much fun to do. Obviously, there is nothing wrong with enjoying our times of praise. But we need to examine our motives: Is our praise flowing from our hearts, or is it coming from our emotions? It is all too easy to enter an emotional roller coaster that lasts only as long as the praise service. Real praise, genuine praise, flows from hearts submitted to God. Such praise will come forth, whether loudly, quietly, or silently, regardless of the emotionalism surrounding us.

REVERENTIAL PRAISE

We can also praise the Lord with a slower pace of music. This type of praise may be a combination of praise and worship. It is often directed toward the Lord and is more prayerful and adoring than declaratory praise. We might say: "Dear Lord, I worship You; I adore You; I praise You."

Adoring praise brings us into the spirit of worship and is closely linked with it. I have heard it said that one must praise the Lord for some time before entering into the spirit of worship, but I believe that if you live a life of praise, you can move into worship very easily.

It is not always fitting to praise the Lord on loud-sounding instruments in a church setting. Sometimes we need to praise Him with a softer, more reverential praise. This is especially important when we are about to enter into a time of worship. A quieter at-

mosphere can help people to quiet their hearts before God so that they can enter into reverential worship.

Sometimes, when you are at home or on the job,
it is good to softly praise the Lord, almost in a whis-
per, throughout the day. This type of praise can draw
you into a sense of intimacy with the Lord, bringing
you more fully into a love relationship with Him.
Because you are in a place where others may not
understand or approve of your loud praise, you can
praise the Lord quietly, with your praise remaining
just between you and your Lord.

Rejoicing Toys

The Pharisees were not happy about the exuber-
ant praise of the disciples and asked Jesus to rebuke
them. He answered them:

> *I tell you that, if these should hold their peace, the*
> *stones would immediately cry out.*   Luke 19:40

The thought of stones praising God may seem
very strange to you, but let me tell you about something that happened to me several years ago. I witnessed some rejoicing toys.

I was asked to help get Christmas toys ready for
the children of low-income families. The used toys
were first picked up from donors all over the county.

The First Key: Praise

My job was to help wash the toys and get them ready for distribution. It disturbed me to see some evil-looking toys coming down the line. I said to the Lord, "These toys look demon-possessed. They look like they could do harm to those who receive them."

The Lord spoke to my heart and said, "Cast the demons out of them."

I was surprised and answered, "Lord, can toys be demon-possessed?"

He said, "Cast the demons out."

Not wishing to make a spectacle of myself around those I was working with, I turned my back to the people and began speaking softly to the pile of toys: "Come out of these toys, you demons. I break your power over them."

A few minutes later I heard some music and couldn't tell where it was coming from. I asked a woman who was working across the table from me, "Where is that noise coming from?"

She answered, "I believe it's coming from that pile of toys."

I stepped over to the pile of toys I had been working with and, sure enough, from somewhere in the pile some very sweet music was issuing forth. It didn't seem to come from just one toy, but was a mixture of sounds from many windup toys, as if they were rejoicing together to the tune of *"He is Lord, He is Lord."*

I was so blessed by that experience that I couldn't contain myself. Praise God for all the wonderful things He is doing in our day. He can even touch toys.

ALWAYS REJOICING

As sorrowful, yet alway rejoicing; as poor, yet making many rich; as having nothing, and yet possessing all things.   2 Corinthians 6:10

King David made some grievous mistakes in his life, yet the Lord called him *"a man after his own heart"* (Acts 13:22). The Psalms make evident to us the fact that David spent a lot of his time praising the Lord. That was the primary thing that made him a *"man after [God's] own heart."* But living a life of praise makes it much easier to obey the Lord in other matters, primarily because a rejoicing heart is more open to God. It is harder for the devil to defeat or sidetrack a joyful Christian, one who is looking to the Lord rather than to his problems or to someone else's gifts. If a joyful person does fail, it is easier for him to find victory, since his heart is ready to rejoice at all times.

LEAP FOR JOY?

Blessed are ye, when men shall hate you, and when they shall separate you from their company, and

*shall reproach you, and cast out your name as evil,
for the Son of man's sake. Rejoice ye in that day,
and leap for joy: for, behold, your reward is great
in heaven: for in the like manner did their fathers
unto the prophets.*   Luke 6:22-23

This doesn't seem to make a bit of sense to the carnal mind. Rejoicing and leaping for joy when trouble comes our way demands that we believe that the Lord is in charge and knows exactly what He is doing. There is no need to weep and wring our hands. When we do things the Lord's way, we can break away from our carnal thinking and find victory.

When we are born again, birthed into the realm of the Spirit, we become spiritual beings. The Holy Spirit works within us to reveal the things of the spiritual realm. This is a great key to being able to successfully live the Christian life, to put into practice what the Lord is telling us to do. Something happens in the heavenlies when we obey the Lord, and we can *"rejoice in that day."*

We can rejoice even when we are being criticized by others. The Lord has given me a ministry of deliverance and healing, and I thank Him for the privilege of being used in this way. When I first began to cast out devils and lay hands on the sick, however, some religious people, who could not accept that the Lord could do these things in our day, accused me of operating under the power of the devil. That always puzzled me. Why do people think that Satan can heal and, at the same time, they are sure that the Lord hasn't healed anyone since the days of the apostles? We quickly learned, as a family, that when someone says something false or unkind about us it's time to praise the Lord. We have been amazed at how well this works in quelling the arguments of the uninformed.

I really don't condemn such people, because they simply don't understand what God is doing. I can remember a time when I didn't understand these things myself. And, even though I have served the Lord for a long time now, I am still learning; I expect to keep right on learning until I depart this life. But until then, I have made up my mind that I will not be controlled by the opinions of the unbelievers or the religious. We have a job to do, and that job must be done in the name of the Lord Jesus, by the power of the Holy Ghost, and through a life filled with joy and praise. These things are crucial for all believers.

JOY IN THE MORNING

For His anger endureth but a moment; in His favour is life: weeping may endure for a night, but joy cometh in the morning. **Psalm 30:5**

One way to get into the habit of rejoicing is to

practice it each morning. When you wake up, start the day right, saying, "Thank You, Lord, for another day to rejoice in, a day to praise You, a day to learn, a day to serve in Your Kingdom." When we are in the habit of rejoicing, it is natural to awaken in the morning with joy in our hearts. You may not always show forth your joy outwardly, but your heart is *"always rejoicing.*

Would you like your life to be filled with good days rather than bad ones? Then take the advice of the Apostle Peter, who wrote:

> *For he that will love life, and see good days, let him refrain his tongue from evil, and his lips that they speak no guile: Let him eschew evil, and do good; let him seek peace, and ensue it. For the eyes of the Lord are over the righteous, and His ears are open unto their prayers: but the face of the Lord is against them that do evil.* 1 Peter 3:10-12

Most people's problems are from the neck up: what they hear, what they see and what they think. There is also a very real snare just below your nose. It is called the mouth. That's where your tongue, that *"most unruly member,"* is found. James warned us that the tongue can not only be *"unruly;"* it can be *"full of poison"* (James 3:8). The Word contains further warnings about the use of the tongue:

63

*Thou art snared with the words of thy mouth, thou
art taken with the words of thy mouth.*

Proverbs 6:2

*Death and life are in the power of the tongue: and
they that love it shall eat the fruit thereof.*

Proverbs 18:21

Once, when we were operating a printing business, some college students came into our office to
ask some questions for a survey they were taking.
They asked, "If you knew you were going to die
today, what would you do?"

I said, "I would start praising the Lord and shouting, so when I got to the gates of Heaven I would be
ready to join all those who are already there praising God." That was the only question they asked
that day. They went out the door in a hurry, and I
never saw them again.

Why does it seem so unusual in our day for
people to praise the Lord and rejoice? When praise
is a way of life, it is not abnormal to praise God, as
Paul and Silas did, under the worst of circumstances.
When praising and prayer become so much a part
of our very existence, it is no more abnormal to
praise the Lord than it is to eat our daily food.

David's life was so full of praise that in the midst
of life's toughest circumstances, he burst forth in
praise. The Psalms are full of David's praise songs,

many of which were written during times of trouble. It was no more unusual for David to trust the Almighty God to kill a giant, a bear, or a lion than it was for him to trust the Lord for His daily provision of food and clothing. Praise is a decision that we must make, and if we fail to do so we will never accomplish all that God has for us.

When you begin to make praise a way of life, the Lord will bring a supernatural manifestation of His approval into your life. Praise is perhaps the greatest safeguard against Satan and his attacks that we can use. When we are praising, we are not complaining. When we are praising, we are not being critical.

For example, as the children of Israel passed through the wilderness on their way to the Promised Land, murmuring and complaining became a way of life for them. There was nothing unusual about their critical attitude toward Moses and Aaron; that was their way of life. It was not strange, then, that they complained about their food and their lack of water. Is it any wonder that they had a shortage of these things? God cannot and will not bless chronic complainers. Do you suppose the Israelites would have had any lack of water if they had continuously praised the Lord? Do you think they would have abhorred the manna from Heaven if they'd had a grateful heart to Almighty God for such a nutritious diet?

Complainers find it very difficult to see anything good in life, whereas those who make praise a way of life find it difficult to meditate upon life's evils. Your whole life looks different when viewed through the eyes of praise. Your spouse, your children, your home, your job — all become more valuable to you when you are praising the Lord in thankfulness for them rather than complaining about them.

No wonder God inhabits the praises of His people! No wonder God shook the prison for Paul and Silas! No wonder their fellow prisoners received salvation! As the psalmist cried out:

> *Oh that men would praise the Lord for His goodness, and for His wonderful works to the children of men!* Psalm 107:8

"IN EVERYTHING GIVE THANKS"

> *Rejoice evermore. Pray without ceasing. In every thing give thanks: for this is the will of God in Christ Jesus concerning you.*
> 1 Thessalonians 5:16-18

At one time this passage was a problem for me, especially the last verse. How can anyone give thanks in everything? But I had been reading it wrongly. I thought we were to give thanks for everything, the bad along with the good, but the Scripture doesn't say that. It says *"in everything,"* not "for everything." This makes quite a difference! When we give thanks to the Lord in the midst of trying circumstances, we are giving the problem to the Lord. That is where it belongs, for He alone can take care of it.

The Lord has worked wonders in our family as we have learned more and more to thank the Lord in everything. It doesn't always make sense to praise the Lord, but it works. Our head wants to protest, because we have been taught to carry our own burdens instead of casting them on the Lord. He didn't just say to give them to Him, He said to *"cast [them] upon Him"*:

> *Casting all your care upon Him; for He careth for you.* 1 Peter 5:7

The word *"casting"* means "to throw." God invites us to throw our cares onto Him, to give them a good toss. Isn't that great? We need not carry those cares around with us day after day. When we are burdened down with care, we have a tendency to get rather upset or disagreeable, but when we put all of our worries on Christ, we don't have those cares any more and have nothing to be upset about. Thank God for His goodness, mercy, and love! He works everything out according to His great wisdom and power. It is the will of God for you to give thanks in every situation.

Ask the Lord to help you as you continue your journey of praise. Endeavor to make praise a life-style, and look to see what the Lord will do in you and through you as you make your life one of praise to His holy Name.

— 4 —

THE SECOND KEY: LIFTING HOLY HANDS

I will therefore that men pray every where, lifting up holy hands, without wrath and doubting.

1 Timothy 2:8

The order in which we present the next keys is of no significance. They are all biblical keys that need to be restored to the Church. And all should flow from a heart of rejoicing, coming forth in sincerity and truth.

This second key, lifting holy hands before the Lord, seems like such a simple thing, yet it can be very hard to do if we allow ourselves to be bound by the traditions that some local churches foster. Lift-

ing up your hands before the Lord may seem to be
strange or unusual to some, but it was a common
practice throughout the Scriptures:

> *Thus will I bless thee while I live: I will lift up my
> hands in Thy name.*   Psalm 63:4

> *Lift up your hands in the sanctuary, and bless
> the Lord.*   Psalm 134:2

There is great power in the lifting of our hands
toward the Lord. When He sees our hands lifted
before Him, it communicates a message to Him. We
are saying: "I can't handle this problem by myself,
so I give it to You." When we bless the Lord and
praise Him with our hands reaching out to Him, we
are surrendering to Him. We are yielding our spirits to His.

The raising of our hands before the Lord is often
overlooked by many believers. They don't seem to
think it is important. Even many who do raise their
hands before the Lord often have no idea of why
they do so. Raising your hands has become a Pente-
costal and Charismatic tradition. But the raising of
hands is mentioned in the Hebrew text of the Bible
more than one hundred times, so obviously, the Lord
thinks it is important. One striking example can be
found in Second Chronicles.

King Jehoshaphat of Judah was a godly man who

looked to the Lord to help him rule his people well. During his reign, the kings of Moab and Ammon came out to fight against him with their great armies. Jehoshaphat knew that he was incapable of facing such a large enemy force, so he gathered all the people together so that they could look to the Lord with prayer and fasting. As they prayed, the king cried out to God, saying, "Lord, we don't know what to do; but our eyes are upon You" (see 2 Chronicles 20:12). The Lord responded by giving Jehoshaphat a plan. Judah would not even need to fight:

> *Ye shall not need to fight in this battle: set your-selves, stand ye still, and see the salvation of the Lord with you, O Judah and Jerusalem: fear not, nor be dismayed; to morrow go out against them: for the Lord will be with you. And Jehoshaphat bowed his head with his face to the ground: and all Judah and the inhabitants of Jerusalem fell before the Lord, worshipping the Lord. And the Levites, of the children of the Kohathites, and of the children of the Korhites, stood up to praise the Lord God of Israel with a loud voice on high. And they rose early in the morning, and went forth into the wilderness of Tekoa: and as they went forth, Jehoshaphat stood and said, Hear me, O Judah, and ye inhabitants of Jerusalem; Believe in the Lord your God, so shall ye be established; believe His prophets, so shall ye prosper. And*

when he had consulted with the people, he ap-
pointed singers unto the Lord, and that should
praise the beauty of holiness, as they went out be-
fore the army, and to say, Praise [yadah] *the Lord;*
for His mercy endureth for ever.

2 Chronicles 20:17-21

The people were to praise God, and that act alone
would win them the battle.

This word *"praise"* is from the Hebrew *yadah*. It
means "to hold out the hand; physically, to throw
something (like a stone or an arrow) at or away; especially to revere or worship with extended hands."
God told the Israel people that they could win the
battle by raising their hands before Him.

"How would the act of raising their hands help
them?" some might ask. I believe that as the people
lifted their hands toward God, they were showing
the Lord their yieldedness to Him. They were ac-
knowledging that on their own there was nothing
they could do to save themselves. Possibly they were
even signifying throwing their enemies away, casting aside their influence. They were also expressing
their thanks to the Lord, in faith that He would move
on their behalf. And they might have been offering
their situation to God as a sacrifice, since the mo-
tion is reminiscent of that used in presenting wave
offerings before the Lord by the priests.

How did God respond to their act of worship?

The Second Key: Lifting Holy Hands

And when they began to sing and to praise, the Lord set ambushments against the children of Ammon, Moab, and mount Seir, which were come against Judah; and they were smitten. For the children of Ammon and Moab stood up against the inhabitants of mount Seir, utterly to slay and destroy them: and when they had made an end of the inhabitants of Seir, every one helped to destroy another. And when Judah came toward the watch tower in the wilderness, they looked unto the multitude, and, behold, they were dead bodies fallen to the earth, and none escaped. And when Jehoshaphat and his people came to take away the spoil of them, they found among them in abundance both riches with the dead bodies, and precious jewels, which they stripped off for themselves, more than they could carry away: and they were three days in gathering of the spoil, it was so much. 2 Chronicles 20:22-25

God brought salvation, victory, and deliverance to His people that day, and not one of the enemy soldiers survived to fight against them again. He also brought them great blessing, for it took them three days to haul away the spoils of battle.

Like Judah, we can win our battles by going forth with our hands raised before the Lord. Certainly, it was more than just the physical lifting of hands that won the battle for the people of Judah that day. It was their heart attitude of submission to the Lord. But that heart attitude was revealed by this simple act of obedience that God had required of them.

When we raise our hands to God, we are saying, "We are helpless and hopeless to meet any enemy, in any situation, in our own strength. But through You and in Your power, we will drive every enemy away. We submit this situation to You, Lord."

Every time we lift our hands to God, He sees them and knows how to fill them with what we need. Many of life's problems wouldn't turn out nearly as bad if we lifted our hands and asked the Lord to work things out for us.

Some people boast of their obedience to the Bible, yet they are the very ones who protest against lifting their hands before the Lord. Such people are deceiving themselves. I have heard well-meaning people speak as though the lifting of the hands was a worldly idea. They seem to believe that it is more important to lift their hands within their spirits than to obey the clear teaching of the Word to physically lift their hands. Such people seek to spiritualize whatever doesn't fit into their traditional teachings. Yet how can they "spiritually" lift their hands in submission and yielding to the Lord, if they will neither submit nor yield to what the Bible asks us to do?

If those people who are reluctant to lift their hands would just try it, they would be surprised at the result. And when one becomes accustomed to doing it regularly, this expression of praise can become a powerful way of reaching out to God to supply our needs.

THE IMPORTANCE OF MAINTAINING CLEAN HANDS

Who shall ascend into the hill of the Lord? or who shall stand in His holy place? He that hath clean hands, and a pure heart; who hath not lifted up his soul unto vanity, nor sworn deceitfully. He shall receive the blessing from the Lord, and righteousness from the God of his salvation.

Psalm 24:3-5

Draw nigh to God, and He will draw nigh to you. Cleanse your hands, ye sinners; and purify your hearts, ye double minded. James 4:8

Since the lifting of our hands before God is so important, we must be sure to maintain clean hands, hands free from defilement. Obviously, this goes deeper than simply using soap and water before we praise the Lord with uplifted hands.

Our hands signify our deeds, the things we do, and God's desire is that we be doing clean things, good things. Our hands are to be full of good works, not dirtied by sin or idleness. Our hands should be washed by the Blood of the Lamb, cleansed for those good works which we will perform in His name.

Holy hands that have reached out to God are hands that the Lord can use. Through them He can lay His hands on the sick, ordain His servants for the ministry, and impart blessing. Through holy hands He can feed the hungry, comfort the afflicted, and strengthen the weary. Empty hands that are clean and pure, hands which are undefiled, gain God's attention and will be filled.

There are many sins that can defile our hands and keep us from ascending the hill of the Lord. If you know you have sinned, lift your hands toward Heaven and say, "I apply the precious blood of Jesus upon these hands. Lord, I ask You to cleanse these hands — in the Name of Jesus." Thank God, we don't have to go around with unholy hands.

A Sacrifice of Praise

Yadah is only one of the words that describes the lifting of hands before the Lord. Another word that is used in Scripture is *towdah*, which is "an extension of the hand in avowal (vows made) or adoration; it also implies confession, a sacrifice of praise, a thank offering." Another meaning for this word is "a choir of worshipers."

In other words, lifting the hands may be considered a sacrifice offered before the Lord, pleasing to

The Second Key: Lifting Holy Hands

Him. We can easily understand that the concept of confession is linked with that of having clean hands. And again we see the idea of being thankful to the Lord, perhaps in faith that He will take care of the situation or circumstance we lift before Him.

It is easy to see that, properly understood, the raising of our hands can be a powerful tool in spiritual warfare. As we give a situation over to the Lord, lifting it before Him as we lift up our hands, we are looking to Him in submission to His will and in faith that He will go before us. We are throwing aside the influence of the enemy over us. We have seen this aspect of the lifting up of our hands at work many times through the years of our ministry, and the Lord has used our obedience in this small matter to bring about great things for us. Whether in our home or at church, whenever we have run into a problem or need special help from the Lord, we have lifted our hands to Him and completely surrendered our will and way to the Lord. What a difference it has made! What joy it is to watch the Lord stop our enemies in their tracks and give us the needed victory!

Once we were told that a number of people had purposed together to destroy our ministry. I had been preaching against adultery and fornication, and this had upset them, even though they called themselves Christians. Apparently they were living in sin with those who were not their spouses. We soon

77

faced the biggest attack our ministry had known until that time.

Our response was simple. We did not know exactly what our enemies planned to do, or how they would come against us, and we were powerless to defend ourselves against the lies they spoke. There was really nothing we could do in the natural. So we did what we could do: We lifted our hands before the Lord, and we prayed. God saw our yieldedness to His will and did a miracle. Supernaturally our enemies were scattered and could not bring to pass the destruction they had planned for us.

My friend, there will be times in your life when you will also find yourself completely helpless against the devil. Know in those moments that you can always win because you are on the Lord's side. Praise Him for His wonderful works to the children of men. Lift your hands in surrender before Him and watch as your enemies scatter in confusion.

— 5 —

THE THIRD KEY:
DANCING BEFORE THE LORD

*Let them praise his name in the dance: let them
sing praises unto him with the timbrel and harp.
For the Lord taketh pleasure in his people: He will
beautify the meek with salvation.* Psalm 149:3-4

A third key to a victorious Christian life is to be
found in the dance. The dance did not originate with
the devil and his crowd, as some might think. God
created it, and it is His wonderful plan that His children express their joy to Him by dancing. David
danced before the Lord on Mt. Zion, and Miriam
and the women of Israel danced before the Lord

79

along the shores of the Red Sea. There are many other examples in the Bible.

Some may say, "Yes, but that was in the Old Testament." While it is true that these examples are from the Old Testament, there is nothing in the Bible, Old or New Testament, to say that the act of worshiping God in the dance was to cease in New Testament times. Dance terms are, in fact, used throughout the entire Bible. It is possible that the negative concept of dancing was already in place, however, by the time the Bible was translated into English, for many terms that referred in the original languages to dancing were routinely translated into English as "praise," "rejoice," "exceeding glad," etc. A true biblical perspective on dancing can be found by studying those passages.

A beautiful example of dance in worship and its origins is found in the writings of the prophet Zephaniah:

> *The Lord thy God in the midst of thee is mighty; He will save, He will rejoice over thee with joy; He will rest in his love, He will joy over thee with singing.* Zephaniah 3:17

This word *"rejoice"* comes from the Hebrew *gul*, and means "to spin around under the influence of a violent emotion." God is dancing and twirling with joy over His people. What a wonderful thought!

The Third Key: Dancing Before the Lord

Just because the devil has corrupted the dance doesn't mean that the Church has to give it up. If a father gives a toy to his children and they get it dirty, does that mean that he must take it away from them and never give it back? Certainly not! Quite likely he will clean it up, show his children how to use it properly, and then place it back in their hands. And so it is with the dance. The world has messed it up, but the Lord is in the business of restoring tarnished things back to His people.

Both instrumental and vocal music have been abused by the world, but that doesn't mean that we should lay them aside and never use them as a means of worshiping God. And the same is true of the dance, which, I believe, God created originally to be an expression of worship.

At the beginning it was difficult for us to teach our congregation about worship in the dance. Dancing was such a taboo within our Christian tradition. But as we sincerely studied the Word of God, we found that dancing before the Lord was not presented as an option. It was a command. When my personal study of the subject brought me to the place of understanding that we dance before the Lord and not before men, the concept suddenly made sense to me.

After our church began to obey the Bible concerning dance, I wrote a song which we have used in our services:

WE WILL DANCE BEFORE THE LORD

We will dance before our Savior,
We will dance before the Lord.
We will dance with joy and gladness,
We will dance in one accord.
We will dance with praise and singing,
We will shout the victory!
We will join our hearts together
As we dance in jubilee.

Dancing, dancing, singing, dancing
As we dance in jubilee.
Dancing, dancing, singing, dancing
As we shout the victory.
Let us lift our voice in triumph,
Let us lift our hands in praise.
Dancing, dancing, singing, dancing
Let the hallelujahs raise!

© 1996 — Daniel D. Rodes

I have found that many people who oppose dancing during church services just don't understand its value. That shouldn't be an impediment, however. Since the Lord's Word, the Bible, instructs us to dance, who are we to disobey just because we don't understand it? Of course dancing, like anything else, must be kept decent and in order or it can lose its value.

The Third Key: Dancing Before the Lord

Our traditions may keep us bound just as securely as Paul and Silas were bound in the prison at Philippi, but just as their shackles fell from them when they began to praise the Lord, so can ours — if we will obey God. We can dance until those traditions fall away from us forever.

Dance is a powerful instrument for breaking through satanic barriers, temptations, doubts, fears and other such hindrances. That is why the devil has fought it so terribly and why it has fallen into such disuse within the Church. He knows that there is great power in dance and will do everything he can to stop Christians from dancing before the Lord.

Dancing before the Lord is a form of rejoicing. It never involves sensuality or an enticement to fleshly lusts. It is a holy act of a holy people before a holy God. As our spirits rejoice before Him, our bodies follow.

MOURNING TURNED TO DANCING

Thou hast turned for me my mourning into dancing: Thou hast put off my sackcloth, and girded me with gladness; To the end that my glory may sing praise to Thee, and not be silent. O Lord my God, I will give thanks unto Thee for ever.

Psalm 30:11-12

One of the weapons the enemy frequently uses

to defeat Christians is the subtle tool of emotion. He brings a spirit of mourning, sadness, or depression upon us. Sometimes the circumstances in which we find ourselves cause this or facilitate this, but our Lord has better things for us and wants to turn our mourning into dancing.

God wants us to throw off that old sackcloth of sorrow and grief and be clothed with gladness. So many people walk around in hurt, anger or self-pity, but we can be joyful, praising believers. What a difference it makes when our hearts are filled with praise and thanksgiving!

Your mourning can be turned into dancing if you will just choose to praise God when your heart is filled with sorrow. Cast off that garment of sorrow, grief, and disappointment, and ask the Lord to gird you with gladness. No matter what the circumstances of your life happen to be, God is in control. So you have every right to rejoice.

Some people become very discouraged because of bills they cannot pay. One of the ways to gain victory over this is to lay your unpaid bills on the floor and rejoice and praise the Lord as you dance around them. If you are not accustomed to doing such things, this may be difficult for you at first. Think of dance as a weapon you are using, not only to gain the upper hand in the matter of your unpaid bills, but also over the discouragement and despondency they have caused. Many people who are suffering from depression or discouragement could be freed simply by obeying this one command.

The physical act of dancing can help to ease depression. The world knows this, and so the people of the world dance. The exercise and the increased levels of oxygen flowing through your body, and just the act of moving in time with the flow of the music, are all good for you. There is, then, a physiological reason to dance. When we use dance as it was created to be used, however, as an expression of worship to our God, the result is much more wonderful than if we simply danced to forget our troubles. We are to *"praise Him with ... the dance"*:

> *Praise Him with the timbrel and dance: praise Him with stringed instruments and organs.*
>
> Psalm 150:4

We do it as an act of worship, but it does us a world of good in the process. Dancing can change our attitudes, lift our heavy burdens, and even help us to receive healing for our bodies. Sometimes when I am ministering I ask those who have been slow to receive healing to dance before the Lord. Those individuals rarely refuse to do it, and they rarely fail to be healed. Time and time again I have seen healing come when people began to dance. Dancing before the Lord is powerful.

THE POWER OF THE DANCE

Dancing before the Lord has been a great blessing in our own lives. One evening Esther, Naomi and I were driving home from a meeting with some friends. It was late, and we had a two-hour drive ahead of us, so the others went to sleep. After we got on the main highway, I began to experience some severe pain all over my body. I started quietly praising the Lord, not wanting to wake them. Esther heard me, however, and, without knowing what was wrong, she began to quietly praise the Lord with me. By the time we got home, my left leg was not responding, and I had difficulty walking. I got into the house and into the bedroom by dragging that leg.

What should I do? My heart wanted to be afraid, and my head wanted to rush to the nearest hospital. But I said, "No! Jesus is my Doctor, and He will give me victory over this." I stood there for a while praising the Lord and, when I didn't seem to be getting better, I said, "Lord, I really don't know what else to do."

He answered in just one word: "Dance."

Dance? I couldn't dance! I could barely move, much less dance. I was determined, however, to be healed, and I was determined to obey the Lord, so I started to move a little — as much as I could. Within minutes, I was feeling better and was shouting and dancing more exuberantly. Before many minutes had passed I was completely healed! That night I became more convinced than ever that dancing has a very important place in the Christian life.

I am grateful for the worldwide ministry the Lord has given us, but sometimes the bills seem to stretch that far as well. There is radio time to be paid, airline tickets and many other costs involved. Just the fact that we are in full-time ministry doesn't guarantee that all the bills will be paid. We must seek God's face. We have found that dancing sometimes helps us receive a breakthrough in this area of finances.

When we wonder how we can pay the ministry bills, we take down the large laminated map of the world, lay it on the floor of the office, and then we dance over and around it. We ask the Lord to meet every need, and we proclaim our faith in His provision. Although I don't understand all of the implications of our dancing in this way, I can testify that the Lord responds every time we do it. I believe that it pleases Him when we express our dependence upon Him through the dance.

DANCE BEFORE THE LORD

Dancing, like any other form of worship, can become vain and useless — if the Spirit of the Lord is not continually operating in our lives. When the children of Israel had turned their backs on God and on Moses, God's leader, they still danced. Now, however, they danced before a golden calf that Aaron had made, not before the living God. We are all responsible for our dancing, to make sure that our hearts are sincere and that we are dancing as unto the Lord. We must take extra care not to become worldly or carnal.

Since dance is a visual ministry, we need to be careful about what it is that we are communicating. Our movements should never be sensual or immodest, but should glorify God.

I caution people against dancing hand in hand with others. Some people insist that this encourages a spirit of unity among the believers, but too much freedom in this area could lead to lust. It seems unwise for men or women to dance with each other. This is just asking for trouble. Don't let dancing become a stumbling block. Avoid *"all appearances of evil"* (1 Thessalonians 5:22). Keep this holy form of worship holy.

"Is it really wise?" some people have asked me, "to encourage dancing in the church since it can be abused, and some people invariably dance 'in the flesh'?" My answer is always yes. Although the possibility exists that some people might dance "in the flesh," at least they're trying to do what the Bible says. They may begin "in the flesh," but if they keep trying, one day they will get "into the Spirit."

The Third Key: Dancing Before the Lord

In truth, however, this term "dancing in the Spirit" isn't even found in the Bible. The Bible speaks of dancing "before the Lord." So dance, and whether you are "in the flesh" or "in the Spirit," I doubt if most people will know the difference. Dance to please God and not man.

People didn't like it when David danced either:

And David danced before the Lord with all his might; and David was girded with a linen ephod. And as the ark of the Lord came into the city of David, Michal Saul's daughter looked through a window, and saw king David leaping and dancing before the Lord; and she despised him in her heart.   2 Samuel 6:14 and 16

David wasn't worried about who was watching him or what they were thinking. He was dancing *"before the Lord."* His dance was not for the nation or for the people or for his wife. It was for the Lord only, and I'm sure the Lord was pleased, whatever others happened to think about it. David was dancing to express his joy and gratitude to the Lord at the return of the Ark of the Covenant to Jerusalem.

I may not be able to dance like David. In fact, I can't keep up with some of the younger people in our congregation. I so admire their ability to worship the Lord in this way, but some of us older folks must recognize that it is difficult to still dance with such skill. Talent or gracefulness or ability, however, are not what matters when it comes to worshiping God. What really matters is our obedience out of a pure heart, as we dance before the Lord, directed and empowered by His Spirit.

If you are just beginning to dance before the Lord, you may feel a little awkward and timid at first. Just remember that you are not dancing before the people or before the church, but before the Lord. That makes all the difference.

Now, dance before the Lord.

— 6 —

THE FOURTH KEY: MARCHING

And ye shall compass the city, all ye men of war, and go round about the city once. Thus shalt thou do six days. And seven priests shall bear before the ark seven trumpets of rams' horns: and the seventh day ye shall compass the city seven times, and the priests shall blow with the trumpets. And it shall come to pass, that when they make a long blast with the ram's horn, and when ye hear the sound of the trumpet, all the people shall shout with a great shout; and the wall of the city shall fall down flat, and the people shall ascend up every man straight before him. Joshua 6:3-5

A fourth aspect of praise and worship that the Lord showed me would bring victory to many is marching. In many churches this expression of praise to the Lord is relegated to the children, who may march as they sing some song of warfare. But the Lord did not intend that marching be just for children. Like the other keys He has given to His people for our use, He wants all of His people to participate. We are all to march in victory before Him.

Marching is both a proclamation of victory and an act of warfare, calling to mind an army marching into battle. The army in which we are enlisted is truly a victorious one, for our battle is already won.

JOSHUA'S MARCH

The most well-known passage concerning marching in the Bible is this one concerning Joshua and the Battle of Jericho. Moses had died and Joshua had come to power when the people finally arrived at the crossing of the Red Sea, ready to enter and take the Promised Land. Jericho would be the first of the Canaanite cities they would face, and the Lord would use the victory there to establish Joshua as His appointed leader over the people.

When Joshua sought the Lord for guidance in the matter, the Lord gave him a unique battle plan:

The Fourth Key: Marching

And the Lord said unto Joshua, See, I have given into thine hand Jericho, and the king thereof, and the mighty men of valour. And ye shall compass the city, all ye men of war, and go round about the city once. Thus shalt thou do six days. And seven priests shall bear before the ark seven trumpets of rams' horns: and the seventh day ye shall compass the city seven times, and the priests shall blow with the trumpets. And it shall come to pass, that when they make a long blast with the ram's horn, and when ye hear the sound of the trumpet, all the people shall shout with a great shout; and the wall of the city shall fall down flat, and the people shall ascend up every man straight before him. Joshua 6:2-5

Although the King James uses the phrases *"compass the city"* and *"go round about the city,"* what the people were doing was marching. They went forth by ranks, as the army of the Lord and of His servant Joshua.

When an army marches forth, its members are focused on what lies ahead. Soldiers marching in rank don't pause to look behind them. They must forget the things they are leaving behind. They don't pause for introspection or self-consideration. They are looking ahead, concentrating on getting to the place of their assigned duty. This is the mind-set of those who march.

When Joshua and his people trusted the Lord and marched forth in obedience, total victory awaited them. It is a classic story:

> *And it came to pass on the seventh day, that they rose early about the dawning of the day, and compassed the city after the same manner seven times: only on that day they compassed the city seven times. And it came to pass at the seventh time, when the priests blew with the trumpets, Joshua said unto the people, Shout; for the Lord hath given you the city. And the city shall be accursed.*
>
> *So the people shouted when the priests blew with the trumpets: and it came to pass, when the people heard the sound of the trumpet, and the people shouted with a great shout, that the wall fell down flat, so that the people went up into the city, every man straight before him, and they took the city. And they utterly destroyed all that was in the city.*   Joshua 6:15-17, 20-21

The people marched, and the people shouted, but it was the Lord who brought forth the victory.

MARCHING FORTH IN JUDGMENT

Marching also may carry an implication of judgment:

The Fourth Key: Marching

Thou didst march through the land in indignation, Thou didst thresh the heathen in anger. Thou wentest forth for the salvation of Thy people, even for salvation with Thine anointed; Thou woundedst the head out of the house of the wicked, by discovering the foundation unto the neck. Selah.   Habakkuk 3:12-13

Here we see a prophetic picture of the Lord marching forward in indignation to bring judgment to the heathen. He also marched to bring *"salvation to [His] people."*

Earlier in the book of Habakkuk, the prophet spoke of God raising up the Chaldeans, who would *"march through the breadth of the land"* and bring the Lord's judgment upon the people (Habakkuk 1:6).

We can march to bring the Lord's judgment upon the works of unrighteousness, upon the strongholds which surround a family, a church, a town or a nation. We can march to demonstrate, before heavenly and earthly realms, that we are the army of the Lord.

When soldiers or guards are trained, part of that training is in marching. There are several reasons for this. Marching builds confidence. As we watch soldiers marching, their backs straight, their heads held high, we can sense the confidence they are building. Something about marching has a powerful effect upon those who participate. Marching exhibits a sense of power that cannot be experienced in mere walking, and that sense of power is reflected to those who observe it.

As you march before the Lord, recognizing that He goes before you and leads you, hold your head up high and go forth, confessing that the One who is in you is great. Remember the words of John:

> *Ye are of God, little children, and have overcome them: because greater is He that is in you, than he that is in the world.* 1 John 4:4

As you march, proclaim the promises of the Word of the Lord:

> *I can do all things through Christ which strengtheneth me.* Philippians 4:13

> *If God be for us, who can be against us?*
> Romans 8:31

> *Not by might, nor by power, but by My Spirit, saith the Lord of hosts.* Zechariah 4:6

> *No weapon that is formed against thee shall prosper; and every tongue that shall rise against thee in judgment thou shalt condemn. This is the heritage of the servants of the Lord, and their righteousness is of Me, saith the Lord.*
> Isaiah 54:17

The Fourth Key: Marching

For the weapons of our warfare are not carnal,
but mighty through God to the pulling down of
strong holds.   2 Corinthians 10:4

There are many other Scriptures that you can sub-
stitute.

One key to being victorious as you march is to be
like those soldiers. Focus on where you are going,
not on where you have been. Look to the Lord, not
to yourself or to your problems. Focus on your Lead-
ership, the One who is ever victorious and cannot
lose a battle. It is as we recognize our complete help-
lessness to save ourselves or to redeem a situation
that the Lord moves to bring us to victory:

When the enemy shall come in like a flood, the
Spirit of the Lord shall lift up a standard against
him.   Isaiah 59:19

The Jewish rabbis have traditionally seen this
verse in a little different way and have placed the
comma in a different spot. Their rendition would
read like this:

When the enemy shall come in, like a flood the
Spirit of the Lord shall lift up a standard against
him.

We can all agree with this! It is the Lord who enters as a flood, not the enemy. The Lord floods every situation with His Spirit and His revelation. We can trust in our God, for He is able to save *"to the uttermost."*

MARCH AROUND THAT JERICHO

Once we were facing some difficulties within our ministry, difficulties which we needed to break through if we were to continue to be effective. As I prayed about them, the Lord spoke to me, reminding me of this passage in Joshua and how he was able to overthrow Jericho by marching around the walls and declaring his promised victory. God told me to go to our church building and to march around it each day for seven days. If I missed a day, I was to begin again. On the seventh day I was to march around the building seven times, as they had at the Battle of Jericho.

Although it seemed a bit silly to me at the time, I did what the Lord was asking. "What good will this do?" my natural mind was asking. But I persisted and, as I marched, the Lord worked in my spirit, preparing me to see what He would do in the situation. My level of expectancy rose with each circuit I made. Finally, on the seventh day, as I marched around the building seven times, I heard the Lord telling me to shout loudly. As I shouted forth at the command of the Lord, I could sense something happening in the spiritual realm. The Lord was bringing us the victory. I knew it. The walls of opposition were beginning to fall down flat.

Outwardly, I could see no immediate change in our situation, but I continued to rejoice in God for what I knew He had done and, although it took several weeks of faithful watching and rejoicing in God, we finally did have a great and unmistakable breakthrough. The Lord had overcome the devil for us because of our obedience.

There have been many other occasions when we have marched around our Jerichos, situations that we needed to overcome by the might of the Lord. We have done this, also, when we faced times of financial need. When funds are slow and there are bills to be paid, we march around those bills proclaiming, "These bills are paid, in the Name of Jesus! The Word of God says, *'My God shall supply all your need.'* These bills are paid!" The Lord always provides.

BLESS THAT CITY

By the blessing of the upright the city is exalted: but it is overthrown by the mouth of the wicked.
Proverbs 11:11

We can also use marching as a means of blessing a city, and when the righteous bless a city, it is blessed. If you have ever heard someone curse God, you know what an effect that has on you. Whether we understand it or not, when evil men curse cities, they are affecting those cities for evil — even if no one hears them doing it. I understand that demon worshipers stand on high hills above cities and towns to curse the people who live there, and the people are unknowingly affected.

What can we do as children of God? I believe that we have a lot more power to bless than we may realize: *"By the blessing of the upright the city is exalted."* I have stood at those same high places where workers of darkness stand to curse and have spoken blessing upon the people and asked the Lord to push back the works of darkness. This type of blessing over a city can make a difference.

We need not curse the demon worshiper. Instead, we are to bless, as Christ taught:

> *But I say unto you, Love your enemies, bless them that curse you, do good to them that hate you, and pray for them which despitefully use you, and persecute you.* Matthew 5:44

When we bless our enemies, we are speaking into their lives the best that God has for them. And what would that be? That they should come to know Him.

Too many people have a wrong attitude toward unbelievers, forgetting that they themselves were once in sin as well. They speak about the wicked in a degrading fashion that places further curses upon them. We cannot agree with the attitudes or deeds of the wicked, but we must keep a holy attitude as we talk about them or pray for them. We can speak blessing into their lives in faith that God will bless them in the best way possible.

When we bless a city, we are speaking into the life of that city. We speak the blessing of God upon it, that the city will prosper, that the righteous there will flourish, and that evil will be restrained. We can help to deliver a city from the evil that binds it. Jesus taught this:

> *Whose soever sins ye remit, they are remitted unto them; and whose soever sins ye retain, they are retained.* John 20:23

In other words, if we are continually discussing all the evil and wrongdoing in a town, a church, or a home, we are retaining those sins that are being committed and helping Satan to keep that place and its people in bondage. What we need to do is *remit*, or release, those who are in bondage, by applying the Blood of Jesus Christ over them and by binding the works of darkness by the authority of God's Word. If we are willing to bless the city rather than cursing it, we will see God's blessing upon it revealed.

Our words have a powerful influence upon others — for good or for evil, and one of the reasons so many Christians are in bondage today is that they take the freedom to slander, gossip, and backbite their fellow believers. The Church must rise up and put a stop to this type of conduct among the people of God. God would not allow it, and neither must we.

Not only are we to bless cities and towns; it is also good to bless our families. The evil of the place they live may be affecting the members of your family in ways of which you may not even be aware. Regardless of your situation, it is best to continually confess the power of the blood of Jesus over your family. Never do this with vain repetitions. Speak the word of faith.

"But what," you may ask, "does all of this have to do with marching?" One effective way to bless a city, church or dwelling is to march around or through it, proclaiming the blessing of the Lord and the release of strongholds. As you march, you are showing the principalities that you are a member of God's army, that you are militant, and that you mean business. One must be careful, however, not to make a display of himself or to have an attitude that would indicate he is taking control of the city. We must operate humbly in the Lord's plan.

If marching around or through a city does not seem to be workable, another approach is to march around a map of the area. We have done this, proclaiming, "We claim this city for the Lord Jesus Christ. By the power of the Blood of the Lamb, we bless this city." Depending on the circumstances and the Lord's leading, we have sometimes done this several times. It is good also to bless the family members of the marchers.

Marching, though not often used by many churches, is one of the keys to victorious living in God. Be obedient to the Lord's calling upon your own life and boldly march forth to victory.

— 7 —

THE FIFTH KEY: SHOUTING

Be glad in the Lord, and rejoice, ye righteous: and shout for joy, all ye that are upright in heart.
                                        Psalm 32:11

From the chariot races of Rome to the jousting tournaments of the knights of ancient Europe, from present-day football games to actual battles, the story has been much the same throughout history. Whenever man badly wants a victory, he always responds with a great shout. And when that victory is gained, he does it again.

Have you ever wondered why men respond as

they do? I personally believe that God Himself has placed the shout within us. After all, He shouts:

> *God is gone up with a shout, the Lord with the sound of a trumpet.* Psalm 47:5

So, if even God shouts, I guess we can too. Shouting can be a powerful weapon of warfare.

Joshua and his people shouted at Jericho. Gideon and his band shouted when faced with the superior forces of the Amelikites. And David shouted as the Ark was being returned to the Holy City. There is power in the shout of victory!

SHOUT FOR VICTORY

Gideon, who was *"the least"* in his father's household, found himself in very difficult circumstances. Israel had sinned before the Lord and had been delivered by Him into the hands of the Midianites. After seven years of great oppression, the sons of Israel were reduced to hiding themselves in caves and dens in the mountains. It is in one of these hiding places that the Bible introduces us to the young man Gideon. He was there trying to thresh some grain in secret for his family so that it would not be stolen from him by the enemy.

Suddenly, an angel appeared to Gideon and told him that he was called by God to be the deliverer of his people. Gideon accepted the challenge and called an army to battle. Over time, his army was reduced, at the direction of the Lord, to a mere handful of men — three hundred to be exact.

Gideon received a battle plan from the Lord. He was to divide his men into three companies. Each soldier was given a torch and an empty pitcher under which to conceal the torch. In what was probably the shortest basic training ever undergone by an army in history, Gideon instructed his men to do exactly what he did:

> *When I blow with a trumpet, I and all that are with me, then blow ye the trumpets also on every side of all the camp, and say, The sword of the Lord, and of Gideon. So Gideon and the hundred men that were with him, came unto the outside of the camp in the beginning of the middle watch; and they had but newly set the watch: and they blew the trumpets, and brake the pitchers that were in their hands. And the three companies blew the trumpets, and brake the pitchers, and held the lamps in their left hands, and the trumpets in their right hands to blow withal: and they cried, The sword of the Lord, and of Gideon.*

Judges 7:18-20

This small army of men, without any normal weapons of warfare, stood still and shouted and played their trumpets with all their might. The result was that they didn't have to fight or even chase after the Midianites. The Lord did all the work:

> *And they stood every man in his place round about the camp: and all the host ran, and cried, and fled. And the three hundred blew the trumpets, and the Lord set every man's sword against his fellow, even throughout all the host: and the host fled to Beth-shittah in Zererath, and to the border of Abel-meholah, unto Tabbath.* Judges 7:21-22

The battle was won by a shout, and Gideon's army chased the enemy as far as Abel-meholah — the meadow of the dance. The place of victory was the place of rejoicing. How wonderful!

David wrote:

> *Rejoice in the Lord, O ye righteous: for praise is comely for the upright.* Psalm 33:1

There can be great power in shouting before the Lord, and it is time for the Church to lay hold of that power. Joshua understood the power of this type of shouting. On each of the first six days he led the people on a march around the city of Jericho, they were silent. Then, on the seventh day, they marched around it seven times. On that last day, however, something else was added. They shouted for joy.

The first six days of the march, as the people traversed the city in silence, must have been unnerving to the inhabitants of Jericho. They could see an entire army led by the priests and the Ark, but no one was saying anything. All that was heard was the haunting cry of the shofars. But on the seventh day, things were quite different:

> *And it came to pass at the seventh time, when the priests blew with the trumpets, Joshua said unto the people, Shout; for the Lord hath given you the city.* Joshua 6:16

We all know the rest of the story. The people of Israel shouted, and the walls fell flat before them. They had won a great victory through their obedience in the shout.

Sometimes there are walls in our lives as well. They may be situations or circumstances or people who are blocking the path the Lord Himself has laid out for us. There are times when it seems we just cannot go around these obstacles in our paths. Somehow, we must plow through them. At times such as these, we may have to shout until those walls fall down before us.

This phenomena can be difficult to understand. What is there about a loud noise that would make strong walls fall flat? The shout of the Lord is a shout of victory. It is a shout of joy in our overcoming God. And it is a shout of faith.

Shouting, like other forms of praise, may be misused. People may shout for any number of reasons. Some may shout to display their authority. Some may shout just because they feel like it. Some may shout in anger or in self-righteousness. Some may shout in an attempt to gain God's attention or to try to force Him to do things their way. None of these are God-pleasing shouts. Let every man examine his heart and know his motives.

SHOUTING DOWN STRONGHOLDS

Shouting the victory is probably most accepted in the area of spiritual warfare. Throughout the Word, and throughout history, we read of men using a battle cry during times of war. We can use shouting in the very same way, as we fight in the spiritual realm.

Shouting is a weapon we can use as we begin to break down strongholds around a city or town. When it is combined with other weapons, such as prayer and fasting, marching, or dancing, it can be powerful. We have seen some wonderful results when we have shouted and commanded that the stronghold of evil be broken in the mighty Name of

Jesus. There is power in the shout — if it is done in faith.

When all else fails, start shouting the victory. Sometimes when we are ministering at a particular church where a breakthrough is needed, we have the people begin to shout: "Hallelujah! Hallelujah! Hallelujah!" This helps to set the people free. In our own church, we have seen that the shout keeps a heavy spirit from overcoming the people.

If you are a child of God, you ought to shout, for you have something to shout about! There is power in the shout if it comes from a heart of rejoicing and gladness.

You might cry out, "Glory, Hallelujah!" or, "Praise You, Lord!" You can shout a Scripture or an affirmation. Or it could be a shout without words. Shout with a faith-filled spirit and watch and see what happens.

"Shout For Joy"

But let all those that put their trust in Thee rejoice: let them ever shout for joy, because Thou defendest them: let them also that love Thy name be joyful in thee.   Psalm 5:11

Be glad in the Lord, and rejoice, ye righteous: and shout for joy, all ye that are upright in heart.
                                                                Psalm 32:11

Let Thy priests be clothed with righteousness; and
let Thy saints shout for joy.   Psalm 132:9

There are many more Scriptures that we could add here. The idea is that we are to shout, not only for warfare, but also for joy. The Psalms, especially, contain this theme. We are to rejoice in our God, and we are to show our joy by shouting.

Many think nothing of shouting at a football game when their team scores. Should we be any less excited about our great and mighty God? Shout forth your joy in your God, for He delights in hearing your praise.

The King Is Coming

We can shout for victory; we can shout in times of warfare; and we can shout for joy as we rejoice in our God. These are all wonderful uses of the shout. But there is one final use of the shout in the Bible:

Cry out and shout, thou inhabitant of Zion: for
great is the Holy One of Israel in the midst of thee.
                                       Isaiah 12:6

Rejoice greatly, O daughter of Zion; shout, O
daughter of Jerusalem: behold, thy King cometh
unto thee: He is just, and having salvation; lowly,

*and riding upon an ass, and upon a colt the foal
of an ass.*   Zechariah 9:9

Our King is coming! Shout the shout of welcome!
Shout the shout of joy! Shout with a voice of gladness,
welcoming the King of kings!

We can shout for His coming, both now, as He has
come into our lives, to be shown in us and through us,
and for His soon appearing. As we look to that day, we
know that we will not be the only ones who shout:

*The Lord Himself shall descend from heaven with
a shout, with the voice of the archangel, and with
the trump of God: and the dead in Christ shall
rise first.*   1 Thessalonians 4:16

Shout with anticipation! Shout unto God!

— 8 —

THE SIXTH KEY:
LAUGHING

Thou wilt show me the path of life: in Thy presence is fulness of joy; at Thy right hand there are pleasures for evermore.   Psalm 16:11

As we have seen, it is God's desire that we rejoice in Him and in the life He has given each of us. Joy underlies each of these *Seven Keys to Victory*. Without a rejoicing spirit, each key becomes merely another legalistic step to follow, while true rejoicing in our God brings life.

The natural outlet for our rejoicing is laughter, and our God wants to fill our mouths with it:

Behold, God will not cast away a perfect
[undefiled, upright] *man, neither will He help*
the evil doers: Till He fill thy mouth with laugh-
ing, and thy lips with rejoicing.   Job 8:20-21

It is natural for us to be filled with laughter and
to rejoice in our Lord. The most common expression
of joy exhibited by those who get saved or baptized
in the Holy Spirit is laughter or tears — or both at
the same time. Some people weep in repentance and
in acceptance of God's will for their lives, but they
may even weep more at the recognition of His kindness and grace. Neither of these can compare with
the weeping produced by the joy of knowing what
God has done for us.

While some weep, others respond with laughter.
They feel happy! They feel light, as though a great
weight had been lifted from them (and, in reality,
that is exactly what has happened). The more these
people come to realize what a great thing has happened in their lives, the more joyful they become —
until the laughter simply bubbles up within them.
Such joy is beautiful to see. And it's contagious.

Some people have gotten away from such expressions of joy, and often this indicates that they have
lost it. They may once have been filled with joy, but
the difficulties they have experienced have gotten
in the way of their rejoicing. Instead of being thank-

ful, they have become bitter and discouraged, focusing on their troubles instead of upon their Lord.

Such people need to look again to the Word of God and to immerse themselves in it. They need to come to know *"the statutes of the Lord"* which are *"right"* and bring *"rejoicing [to] the heart"*:

> *The statutes of the Lord are right, rejoicing the heart: the commandment of the Lord is pure, enlightening the eyes.* Psalm 19:8

By understanding God's statutes, I mean understanding God's way of doing things. Jesus said:

> *If ye love Me, keep My commandments.*
> John 14:15

Keeping God's commandments, keeping His statutes, becomes the path to true rejoicing.

When asked what the greatest commandments were, Jesus replied:

> *Jesus said unto him, Thou shalt love the Lord thy God with all thy heart, and with all thy soul, and with all thy mind. This is the first and great commandment. And the second is like unto it, Thou shalt love thy neighbour as thyself. On these two commandments hang all the law and the prophets.* Matthew 22:37-40

A life lived according to these commandments is a life that is fulfilled. If we love the Lord first and our "neighbor" second, we will have something to rejoice about.

There are many Christians who are sad and depressed. They face the world from a stance of gloom or despair. Some can sit in a meeting where those around them are laughing and rejoicing in the Lord, yet they will not even smile. These believers are in bondage and need to be set free. God did not ordain such a life for any of His children; His plan is that we rejoice in Him.

Many marriages have been destroyed because one spouse was unhappy and downcast. If there is strife in your marriage, find something to laugh about. Laughter will change your attitude toward your spouse. You can then pray and ask the Lord for His help with all your marital conflicts.

The lives of your children will be brightened if they hear your joyous laughter. One day, when we were having family devotions, I made up a little rhyme about nature rejoicing in the Lord:

NATURE REJOICES

Little tiny raindrops
Dancing on the roof,
They seem so full of glee.
Here's a little proof.

The Sixth Key: Laughing

You can hear them giggle,
Sliding down the spouting.
It is time we Christians
Learned to stop a-pouting!

It was just a simple, rather silly rhyme, but it helped to remind our children that we had reason to rejoice.

Freedom's Laughter

For there they that carried us away captive required of us a song; and they that wasted us required of us mirth, saying, Sing us one of the songs of Zion. How shall we sing the Lord's song in a strange land? Psalm 137:3-4

A Song of degrees. When the Lord turned again the captivity of Zion, we were like them that dream. Then was our mouth filled with laughter, and our tongue with singing: then said they among the heathen, The Lord hath done great things for them. The Lord hath done great things for us; whereof we are glad. Psalm 126:1-3

What a difference there is between these two psalms! In the first, the children of Israel simply could not force themselves to sing the Lord's song, yet in the second, they were filled with laughter and singing. Why such a difference? In the first, they were a people in bondage, while, in the second, they had been set free.

Freedom from bondage makes all the difference in this regard. These days, our problem is probably not a literal bondage to a foreign nation, but we may still be bound. We might walk in bondage to a particular sin or to a tradition. We might be bound by an unwise promise or to the consequences of sin, such as sickness or poverty. There are many types of bondage in the world, but there is One who holds the key to freedom for all of us, and it is He who promised:

> *If the Son therefore shall make you free, ye shall be free indeed.* John 8:36

What a promise! The Lord Jesus holds the key to freedom for each one of us!

There are times when we must be willing to use the key the Lord hands us if we want to taste true freedom. Many Christians are in captivity through pondering all the bad things that happened to them years ago. They dwell on how they were hurt or betrayed and by whom, continually recalling again and again their troubles. No wonder Jesus said:

> *No man, having put his hand to the plow, and looking back, is fit for the kingdom of God.*
> Luke 9:62

The Sixth Key: Laughing

We are not to look back to the things of the past. Rather, we are to look to Him who is our Lord. Looking to the past brings its own captivity. Looking to our God brings laughter, songs, and joyous freedom.

I love to watch people who are being set free from bondages in their lives. They are so happy that it is a joy just to watch them! As we minister, we are seeing more and more of the joy of the Lord expressed through laughter. What a blessing! And what a great testimony to a sad, depressed, joyless world!

HOLY LAUGHTER?

Sometimes I am asked my opinion of the "holy laughter" associated with some of the revival movements we are currently experiencing. I am rather amused when people ask, "But don't you think the people are laughing in the flesh?" Certainly, there are those who laugh in the flesh in those meetings. When this question is asked, I try to ask one in return: "In your church, if your preacher says something humorous, do you laugh?"

When they say they do, I ask, "And do you laugh in the Spirit or in the flesh?" That usually settles the question of whether laughter is holy or not.

Many of those who laugh may only be imitating what they see others do. Some may even be trying to force certain things to happen in their services. Or they may be trying to get what others have received. I don't mean to dismiss legitimate concern about what is happening in certain circles, but I have encountered far too many people who are just critical of laughter of any kind.

Laughter may not always be a sign of joyfulness in some revival meetings, but we cannot stop laughing merely because someone may judge us to be "in the flesh." It is the job of the local church leaders, not the critics, to correct anything in our churches that may not be for edification.

INAPPROPRIATE LAUGHTER

I have personally been in services where people created disturbances by trying to force laughter inappropriately. Laughter, like anything else, must be done *"decently and in order"* (1 Corinthians 14:40). We must be careful not to let laughter or anything else get out of hand, for the devil wants to confuse us and to misuse our blessings so as to give the enemies of God a reason to blaspheme the power and working of our Lord.

There is a proper and an improper use of laughter, and Christ came to set us free from all things that offend. But if we cannot laugh when it is appropriate, we need to rethink our doctrines and lay aside what we have been taught, in order to embrace the new things God is doing among His people.

Why is it that so many people are afraid of new

things? If there is a genuine fear that we might cause some believers to sin by indulging in an unscriptural activity, then we must examine carefully the Word of God and be persuaded in our own minds.

The Bereans were commended, in New Testament times, for their willingness to learn new things:

> *These were more noble than those in Thessalonica, in that they received the word with all readiness of mind, and searched the scriptures daily, whether those things were so.*　　　Acts 17:11

We should take a lesson from the Berean believers. While it is not wrong to be cautious of new things, we must not allow our traditions to keep us from what God wants to do in our lives.

LAUGHTER AND HEALING

There is a connection between laughter and healing. Laughter promotes physical health and healing, a fact that even the secular world has come to recognize. It is also obvious to the medical world that laughter promotes mental and emotional health. Many studies have proven this fact. Rejoicing, including laughter, promotes both of these and spiritual health as well. God wants His people to be full of joy and gladness, and it is to our benefit to accept His will.

There have been times, as we were ministering, that we noticed a spirit of sadness coming over the people. Every time it has happened it has cut off the power of God for healing. God will not operate where there is a spirit of sadness, unless it is for repentance or grief for some time of tragedy. A spirit of sadness or depression will not only keep a person from being healed, it will make them more prone to sickness and disease.

Sometimes, when I ask afflicted people to praise the Lord for their healing, they refuse. I notice that people like that have such a sad and gloomy look on their faces. They will probably never get healed. Others, who are willing to rejoice and thank the Lord, even before the healing is manifested, usually receive a quick healing.

In one of our healing crusades a woman became very disturbed and began to complain: "Everyone is getting healed but me. I don't understand!" She stood there with tears rolling down her face as though God had completely forsaken her. But He hadn't. She had been the only person present who refused to rejoice in the Lord. I saw her some months later and she told me she was healed before she left the meeting place that night. I marvel at the mercy of God.

A merry heart doeth good like a medicine: but a broken spirit drieth the bones.   Proverbs 17:22

124

The Sixth Key: Laughing

There are many different kinds of medicines on the market. Most of them are expensive, and some of them cause serious side effects. There is one medicine that is neither costly or potentially dangerous to your health. It is laughter. It will do you good every time. Laughter can keep you well — physically, mentally and emotionally.

One time I had hiccups that I couldn't seem to get rid of. After praising the Lord for some time and still finding no relief, I asked Him what I should do. His response was just one word: "Laugh."

I said to my family, "The Lord said for us to laugh, so let's all laugh together." At first, nothing seemed to be very funny, but before long we were bursting with laughter. And immediately the hiccups were gone. Since that time, we have used this remedy on a number of occasions.

Another time I had a kidney stone and was lying on the couch groaning in severe pain. Esther was praying for me, and she said, "Dear Lord, my husband will die and not live." She had accidentally misquoted Psalm 118:17, which says, *"I shall not die, but live, and declare the works of the Lord."* This slip of the tongue seemed so funny to me that I burst out laughing in spite of the pain. I laughed so hard that the pain stopped almost immediately. Surely laughter *"does good like a medicine."*

If you have a physical ailment, it may be helpful to use an object lesson to help yourself to laugh and to free you from the bondage of thinking about your problems. I sometimes tell people to get a medicine bottle and fill it with something good-tasting that won't spoil. They are to take a teaspoon of this "medicine" three times a day. Immediately after each dose, they are to shout, "Hallelujah!" and laugh three times. This may seem like complete foolishness, but it can help you to begin to rejoice in God.

Take a little time out to laugh each day. Rejoice in the Lord. Laugh for the joy of the Lord! This is an important key to a beautiful — and happy — life in God.

LAUGHTER AS A REMEDY FOR EMBARRASSMENT

Most of us react very badly when we are embarrassed about something, but it need not be so. One day some relatives were driving my wife and me to a speaking engagement. After we had been on the road for about an hour, I glanced down at my shoes, only to discover that in my haste to get ready for the meeting, I had put on two shoes which didn't match.

At first, I was very embarrassed by what I had done, but the more I thought about it, the funnier it seemed to me. I began to laugh and had to explain my predicament to the others in the car.

When it came my turn to minister, I walked calmly to the front of the church. I had decided to point out to the people what I had done. We all had a good laugh, and I definitely had everyone's attention from that moment on. I suppose I could have been very upset about having to preach in unmatched shoes, but I chose to have a good laugh over it instead. And it worked to my advantage.

Once, on a trip to Canada, I was taken by surprise with the bitter cold. I hadn't taken enough warm clothing along. I decided to wear my pajamas under my suit as an extra layer of protection from the cold nights. The legs of my pajamas were longer than the cuffs of my pants, so I rolled them up, and that seemed to work fine. After the service, however, as I was talking to a few of the people, I glanced down to find that my light blue pajamas were now hanging out several inches below the cuffs of my pants. My first reaction was one of deep embarrassment, but I knew that wasn't the right reaction and decided to make a joke out of it. When I did, I got happy.

When you are full of the joy of the Lord, you can rejoice when you otherwise might have been sad or embarrassed. When you laugh at yourself, others will laugh with you. Joy is contagious.

Another time, when we were living on a farm in Pennsylvania, my sons were helping me gather wood for our woodstove. It was a very strenuous job. The wood had to be cut and split, loaded onto a truck and then unloaded in our woodshed. Because the steel bed of the truck was rather slippery, I got a brilliant idea. Why not just stop the truck suddenly and let the whole load slide off, rather than unload it by hand one piece at a time?

I told the boys to stand back, then I dropped the tailgate and pulled the truck up a good distance away from the woodshed. I put the truck into reverse and began to back up, picking up speed as I went. My intent was to hit the brakes quickly and allow the wood to slide off. *Nothing to it,* I thought. *This will save a lot of work.* When I hit the brakes hard, the pressure caused the brakes to fail. Instead of unloading our wood, I backed right through the side of the woodshed.

I was so shocked that I didn't know what to say, and the boys just stood staring at me, too. Esther, hearing the crash, came to see what had happened. She was also astonished and looked to me for some explanation of why the truck was sitting in the woodshed. I was so embarrassed and surprised that all I could say was, "We wanted the wood in the woodshed, didn't we? Well, there it is." But, after all of that, we still ended up unloading the wood by hand.

We all began to laugh as we planned how to repair the building. We could have endured a discouraging day of strife between us as a couple, and I could have been angry with myself for having caused such a freak accident. But it all turned out to be a fun experience, even with the extra work it caused.

On one occasion, many things seemed to be going wrong within our ministry. Several of our people were not feeling well, and things in the office were not running smoothly. Our ministry vehicle was in the shop, so I took a van and went to run an errand. While I was out, the van's radiator hose burst with a loud bang. Since I was at a distance from the office, I called to ask if someone could come and bring me back. One of our workers agreed to use his own car to come and get me. As he was getting in the car, however, he hit his head so hard on the side of the door that he was bleeding. To top it all off, his car wouldn't start, and the battery had to be charged.

By this time, everyone had begun to laugh, and that changed everything. After everyone had a good laugh, we all started to feel better, and all our problems were settled before nightfall. What could have been a day of total disaster turned out to be a day of rejoicing in the Lord.

LAUGHING RELIEVES FRUSTRATION

It really doesn't pay to get angry with yourself or others over mistakes. If we can keep a cheerful attitude, we can learn from our mistakes. If we get upset and frustrated, we will cause ourselves more problems than ever.

One of the best cures for frustration is to praise the Lord. Laugh at your troubles. If it's possible, stop whatever you are doing that is making you frustrated and spend some time in worship. It won't be long until you begin to feel much better. All of us are affected when someone around us is frustrated, but the atmosphere is completely changed when we choose to be happy instead.

My friend, when you make rejoicing and praising the Lord a way of life, it is a very rewarding experience. Things don't look nearly so bad when there is joy in our hearts. Give glory to God, for He fills our heart with gladness and our mouths with laughter.

— 9 —

THE SEVENTH KEY: WORSHIPING

Then saith Jesus ... it is written, Thou shalt worship the Lord thy God, and Him only shalt thou serve. Matthew 4:10

The final key to experiencing a victorious Christian life is worship. Each of the other keys may be seen as expressions of praise or worship. Each may tend toward one or the other during a given experience. But worship — adoring the Lord and laying oneself before His feet — is also a separate key of its own. Just as we must make time and make the effort to practice the other keys, so we must do with worship.

For we are unto God a sweet savour of Christ, in them that are saved, and in them that perish: To the one we are the savour of death unto death; and to the other the savour of life unto life. And who is sufficient for these things?

2 Corinthians 2:15-16

Our lives are to be fragrant with worship to the Lord. We are an aroma *"of life unto life"* before Him. Worship is not just something we do; it permeates our attitudes, becoming part of who we are.

Many people find it comparatively easy to praise the Lord, but to worship Him can be more difficult. It takes faith to enter into true worship. We can never experience the sense of the presence of the Lord based on *our* righteousness. We can only enter in on the basis of *His* righteousness.

If you have a guilty conscience, you may be able to praise the Lord to a certain extent, but you cannot truly worship Him. Why do I say that? Because worship is more intimate and more personal than praise. Therefore, worship is nearer to the heart of God.

WORSHIP IN SPIRIT AND IN TRUTH

When Jesus spoke to the woman at the well in Samaria, He gave us some important principles for worship. He said:

The Seventh Step: Worshiping

But the hour cometh, and now is, when the true worshippers shall worship the Father in spirit and in truth: for the Father seeketh such to worship Him. God is a Spirit: and they that worship Him must worship Him in spirit and in truth.

John 4:23-24

How wonderful it is to know that our heavenly Father is actually searching through the Earth to find those who will worship Him! But He is not just looking for any old "worshiper" who may think to call on His Name. He has set some standards for those who choose to worship Him: They must worship Him *"in spirit and in truth."*

What does it mean to worship *"in spirit and in truth"*? Well, worshiping *"in truth"* seems fairly simple to understand. We need to speak the truth in the things we say or sing as we worship. If we sing that He is precious, then He should be precious to us, enthroned in our hearts. If we say that we will follow Him wherever He will lead us, then we must mean what we say.

On another level, worshiping in truth means that we are truly worshiping. Our minds are not on anything else but the Lord. Our praise and adoration are for Him and Him alone. Our worship is not divided, but our hearts, our thoughts, and our minds are stayed on Him.

Jesus condemned the worship of the Pharisees, for they did not worship *"in truth"*:

> *Howbeit in vain do they worship Me, teaching for doctrines the commandments of men. For laying aside the commandment of God, ye hold the tradition of men.*   Mark 7:7-8

What was wrong with the worship of the Pharisees? They had laid aside the Scriptures in order to accommodate men's teachings. They could not worship Him *"in truth"* because they were not *of* the truth.

And what does it mean to worship God *"in spirit"*? This means that our worship goes beyond the words that we say or the songs that we sing. It goes deeper than any of the expressions of worship we may use. When we worship *"in spirit,"* our spirit is communicating with His Spirit. In this way, we can touch the very heart of God, and in this way, He can touch our hearts. This communication between mortals and Almighty God is what makes worship so wonderful.

Some people seem to think that we can come before God in a casual manner and that the Lord doesn't care how we worship Him — as long as we are sincere. There is a problem with that theory: Jesus didn't say the Father was looking for sincere people to worship Him. He is looking for those who will worship Him *"in spirit and in truth."* This is not a casual approach, but rather an honest and reverent realization that we are in the presence of the great God of the universe. He is the Creator God, the holy and awesome I AM. We must purpose to come before Him in reverence and humility. We cannot just barge into the throne room of God on our own merits!

A Spirit of Worship

In recent years, the Church has been flooded with teaching concerning worship, and more and more people have begun to lay hold of the teachings on this all-important subject. Undoubtedly, much truth that had been lost to the Church in the area of worship has been restored. Yet, despite all the teachings done in all the worship conferences that have been conducted and the many tapes that have been duplicated and reviewed over and over again, I feel that we still fall far short of what our heavenly Father desires of us in our worship. It is still possible to go through the motions of worship, while our hearts are far from the true spirit of worship.

Through Isaiah, the Lord spoke to the people of Israel:

Wherefore the Lord said, Forasmuch as this people draw near me with their mouth, and with their lips do honour me, but have removed their heart far from me, and their fear toward me is taught by the precept of men. Isaiah 29:13

Surely, if any group of people has known how to worship the Lord, it is Israel. The people of Israel learned their worship from Moses and David. Still, with all their external correctness, the Lord was not pleased with their worship. Their hearts were *"far from [God]."*

When we come to the Lord in worship, our attitude must be one of humility. We must come recognizing our total dependence on Him and allow Him to teach us how to worship in an acceptable manner.

Then we must continue to develop in our worship and praise until we have learned to walk in the fullness of His glory, ever reaching out for a deeper and more meaningful relationship with our great God. The more we yield ourselves to Him, the more we will see the manifestations of the Holy Spirit operating in our lives. And the more He is evident within us, the more will we bring Him glory.

We need to walk softly when we come before the Lord in worship. We are not doing Him a favor by worshiping Him, and we cannot enter into worship if we come thinking too highly of ourselves. We cannot look to any righteousness of our own. We cannot look to the "rightness" of our worship, nor to our skill in expressing our devotion to God. We must come in humility, looking to our Lord, setting our minds on Him, on who He is, and on what He has done and will do.

When you worship, let your mind dwell on God. He is our Savior and has saved us from our sins. Christ *"ever lives to make intercession for us."* He will *"receive us to Himself; that where He is, there we may be also."* He is faithful to us, and we worship Him because He is God. We glorify Him and honor Him. He is so wonderful, so loving, so kind, so merciful, so precious. He is a forgiving God, holy and just. He is the Alpha and Omega, the First and the Last. He is the only true and living God, the Prince of Peace, the Bright and Morning Star. Christ Jesus is *"the Way, the Truth, and the Life."*

We worship Him who is the Light of the World, our Redeemer, our Salvation. Baal failed, and he is no more. Diana, the goddess of the Ephesians, is all but forgotten. But our God is alive forevermore. His dominion knows no limits. His wisdom has no equal. He is omniscient, omnipotent, omnipresent and full of glory.

He is all of these and more. It is no wonder then that when we see Him in the realms of the Spirit, we fall down at His feet and worship Him from the heart.

Let us make such worship a way of life, for our Lord is worthy of all praise and honor and glory!

Hindrances to Worship

There are many things that may become hindrances to worship. One of them is the presence of unrepented sin in our lives. Sin separates us from God and brings us guilt and condemnation. We cannot have the freedom to worship until we have repented of our sins and been cleansed by the blood of Christ.

Some people have told me that even though they are living in sin, they are not hindered from worshiping the Lord. That is difficult to accept, since it is contrary to the clear teachings of the Scriptures. When we serve sin, we are serving the devil. How can anyone claim to be worshiping the Lord and the devil at the same time? While it is true that when we bow down before a holy and righteous God, we come to Him based on His righteousness and not our own, God cannot and will not accept worship from a corrupt heart. He is a holy God, and He expects worship from a holy people. He has said:

Be ye holy; for I am holy.   1 Peter 1:16

If we have guilt or a sin consciousness plaguing us, it is extremely difficult for us to enter into a true worship experience with the Lord. Once our sins have been dealt with by the blood, however, we need never be tormented by them again. The precious blood of Jesus cleanses and sanctifies us, enabling us to come into the presence of the Lord without fear. What peace! What love! What joy! And what forgiveness comes from the presence of the Lord! When we experience this intimacy with God, we can pour out our love and devotion to Him, and nothing on Earth is quite so precious as the knowledge that nothing stands between us and our heavenly Father. What a wonderful privilege to fall at the feet of Jesus and worship!

Cares and worries may also hinder us from worshiping God. We may try to worship, only to be distracted by other concerns. If this happens, we should place our cares in the hands of our Lord, perhaps during a time of praise. We can give all such things to Him, knowing that He cares for us and that He will take care of everything that we place in His hands. Then we can set our minds and hearts on the Lord, knowing that He is in control of all things.

Another enemy of worship is time. It is difficult to worship God if we are pressed for time. If that is the case, we must ask the Lord to show us when we can set aside time to worship Him. Time spent with God must be a priority for us. After all, nothing else we do could be as important as spending time with Him.

God knows what we must get accomplished each day, and time spent with Him will often help us to

better order our other priorities in life. As the psalmist wrote:

My times are in Thy hand.   Psalm 31:15

Another hindrance to worship is church tradition,
those things we have been taught since childhood.
This hindrance can be hard to combat, since we may
feel that if we change we are going against the teaching of the Church. But at some point we must make
a distinction between the teachings of a church and
the teachings of the Word of God. If we want the
blessing of the Lord upon our lives, and we want to
come into intimacy with Him, we must learn to do
things His way, not man's way. Tradition has so
blinded the minds of many people that they fear and
reject any "new thing" God is doing.

Visitors have sometimes walked out of our services because they did not believe in dancing or
shouting in church. But if we always try to please
men, we will wind up displeasing the Lord. If we
want the blessing of the Lord, we must walk in obedience to all that He has shown us to do, and God's
ways can be very different from the traditions we
have been taught.

We should be careful not to judge those who dis-
agree with us. We must love them and pray for them.
Most of them are acting on what they have been

taught and are trying to please the Lord as tradition has taught them to do.

At the same time, we must also be careful not to accept the criticism of those who would lead us away from what God is doing in this day. We cannot judge this move of the Spirit by what the "experts" have to say. Rather, we must judge all things by an honest interpretation of the Scriptures.

Churches and congregations have split over doctrine. We have crippled unity with traditions, and we have built diverse denominations over philosophies. But when it comes to worship, we all end up at the same place — the feet of Jesus.

COMPLETE IN CHRIST

O come, let us worship and bow down: let us kneel before the Lord our maker. For He is our God; and we are the people of His pasture, and the sheep of His hand. **Psalm 95:6-7**

The Lord has made us. He has a right to expect us to bow down and worship Him. Oh, what we have missed by not learning to worship Him long ago! Worship is not an option; we must worship our God if we are to know a victorious Christian life.

We tend to think of worship as something that ministers to God and, in one sense of the word, we are right, for it does. But worship is not a one-way blessing. The Lord does not command our worship just to build up His ego. Worship ministers to us as well. We were created to worship, and we will only be fulfilled when we learn to do so.

We are each far from perfect, but when we learn to worship God, He fills up that which is lacking in our lives. He fills the emptiness in our hearts and satisfies our deepest longings. He fills our hearts with His love, and we begin to take on His nature, His likeness, His character. In the process, we become even better worshipers. The more we worship, the more we want to worship.

We should never let a day pass without spending some time in worship. It is good to praise, and praise is a very important part of Christian life. Yet we must also learn the true meaning of worship and loving devotion to the King of kings and Lord of lords.

Worship And Revelation

Once, when I was worshiping at our church, the Lord gave me a vision. I saw a brazen altar a few feet in front of me. A book was lying on the altar. This book was blazing, with shafts of golden light bursting forth from it.

As I looked, a priest dressed in his robes came up to the side of the altar. He was carrying a Bible with him. He looked at the book on the altar. Then, with disdain, he opened the Bible he was holding in his hand, tore out a page and threw it on the floor. He looked again to the book on the altar. Then he turned a few more pages in his Bible, tore out some more pages, and threw them down. This happened several times. I noticed that every time he looked at the book on the altar, something seemed to make him angry, and he would tear out another page from the Bible he was holding.

Then my eyes were drawn to his garment. Every time he had torn out a page from the Bible, his garment had became more soiled. Now it was literally covered with dirt.

As the priest walked away from the altar, I saw another man approaching it. This man lovingly picked up the Book that lay there and embraced it, holding it to his bosom. When he did, the Book disappeared inside him. The shafts of light that had been coming from the Book as it lay on the altar began to burst forth from him instead. When the man opened his mouth to speak, the golden light would burst forth from his mouth. Then, just as suddenly as it had appeared, the vision faded.

The Lord said to me, "Those who follow men's traditions rend the Scriptures. They teach only a part of My Word. They are polluted and will not heed My end-time message. Those who love the truth will know the truth. The man who picked up My Word received the whole Word into his heart. He is one of My end-time messengers, one of those who will speak the Word and will have greater power and revelation than have been seen in any other time in the history of all Christendom."

After seeing this vision, I cried out, "Oh, Lord, let me be one of those who have the shafts of light coming out from them to preach the glorious Gospel as You want it to be preached in these last days!"

He answered me, "I want you to take the Truth across the world."

As a result of the revelation we received that day, we soon began to increase our broadcasts of the Gospel by radio into a hundred and sixty-eight different countries, a ministry that continues to this day. God's mighty power quickly became evident in our broadcasts and many people were delivered from sin and satanic bondage. We also witnessed dramatic changes in our own congregation after that vision came to me during worship. I marvel at the grace and mercy of God.

Because we were in a spirit of worship that day, we were able to see what the Lord was about to do in our own church circle. Otherwise we might have missed the Lord's plan.

Worship and Prayer

Prayer is vitally important to the Christian, and each of us must develop a prayer life. If we fail to understand praise and worship, however, we can never fully understand prayer. The more we praise and worship the Lord, the deeper and more meaningful our prayer life becomes. There is a proper way to approach God:

> *Enter into His gates with thanksgiving, and into His courts with praise: be thankful unto Him, and bless His name. For the Lord is good; His mercy is everlasting; and His truth endureth to all generations.*   Psalm 100:4-5

God is looking for thankful, praising people to come before Him. We are to *"bless His name."* The Hebrew word for "bless" here is *barak*, which means "to salute, thank, kneel before or give adoration or worship." This is how we are to enter into our times of intimacy with God.

Worship becomes a very powerful and beautiful instrument in reaching the highest potential of intercessory prayer. A true worshiper has an unlimited Source of power, and when we are in the spirit of worship, we are able to express from the heart things we had not even known to pray for. If we could spend more time in worship, putting on the mind of Christ, we might save ourselves from some of the battles we sometimes are forced to wage.

After Esther and I made a decision to worship the Lord freely, I noticed that my prayer vocabulary was changing dramatically. I suddenly found myself talking to God with a power I had never known before. Only the Holy Spirit could have given me such words. Sometimes my prayers were like psalms flowing forth from my innermost heart, expressing to God the needs of the people. There were beautiful expressions of dependence upon an awesome and mighty God, a God full of majesty. And when we spent time in intense praise and worship, God always responded to us in great power and love.

None of us knows how to reach our highest potential in prayer, but when we begin to worship the Lord and lean heavily upon Him for words to speak, we quickly see a difference. Our weak prayers of the flesh are turned into powerful prayers in the Spirit. God becomes great, and our problems become very small.

As we seek Him, the Lord is revealing to us more and more of the secrets of worship that have been hidden for years because we were blinded by the traditions and doctrines of men. Thank God that many are breaking away from the bondage of dead religion into the glorious liberty of true worship. Let us each eagerly accept and practice what the Lord is showing us to do.

Since a heart of worship is necessary for the believer who wants to know intimacy with God, and since it is the key that holds all the others, let us now continue our study of worship and its many facets.

PART THREE:

THE LIFE OF WORSHIP

— 10 —

PROPHETIC WORSHIP

*My soul shall be satisfied as with marrow and fat-
ness; and my mouth shall praise Thee with joyful
lips.*   Psalm 63:5

*Thou wilt show me the path of life: in Thy pres-
ence is fulness of joy; at Thy right hand there are
pleasures for evermore.*   Psalm 16:11

There is a realm of prophetic worship that we can
reach in God, something for which we should all
strive. Prophetic worship comes when we get closer
to God and sense more greatly His presence.

Many don't understand what we mean by being
in the presence of the Lord. Since the Lord is always

present, by being in His presence we mean that we can feel His nearness, and we know that He is with us. It doesn't mean that God just showed up, for He is always with us. In one sense, we are always in the presence of the Lord, for He has promised never to leave us. David wrote:

> *Whither shall I go from thy spirit? or whither shall I flee from thy presence? If I ascend up into heaven, thou art there: if I make my bed in hell, behold, thou art there. If I take the wings of the morning, and dwell in the uttermost parts of the sea; Even there shall thy hand lead me, and thy right hand shall hold me.* Psalms 139:7-10

So when we speak of coming into His presence, what we really mean is that we are recognizing that presence. We have knowledge of it. We sense it. This is all-important to prophetic worship, where our hearts touch His.

My wife and I haven't had a bad day together in many years. We enjoy each other and enjoy being with each other. We spend a great deal of time together, traveling together, talking together, laughing together. We love each other so much that I talk about my wife to other people. And the more I talk about her and praise her to others, the more intimate our relationship becomes. Because of our years of devotion to each other, we share a special intimacy between us.

This same thing can happen in our relationship with the Lord. When we love to come before Him and pour out our hearts to Him, when we learn, by the Spirit, how to express our love and devotion to Him, and, as we walk in what He shows us from day to day, we develop a very special relationship that opens up Heaven's very best blessings to us.

Truly worshiping the Lord brings God's favor upon our lives. We have seen this in the accounts of people in the Bible who praised God in times of difficulty: Jehoshaphat and the people of Israel, Paul and Silas, Joshua as he came against Jericho. This favor of the Lord can be ours as we face our battles, too:

> *A good man obtaineth favour of the Lord.*
>
> Proverbs 12:2

Have you ever wondered why some people seem to be more favored of the Lord than others? Is He showing favoritism? Or could it be that those who are more highly favored have developed a much closer relationship with the Lord?

The psalmist desired the favor of the Lord:

> *I entreated Thy favour with my whole heart: be merciful unto me according to Thy word.*
>
> Psalm 119:58

We should each seek the favor of the Lord. Many people miss it because they don't understand that it is available to them. The favor of the Lord is prepared for those who seek God with a pure heart, rather than seek earthly rewards:

> *For Thou, Lord, wilt bless the righteous; with favour wilt Thou compass him as with a shield.*
>
> Psalm 5:12

Worship always results in blessing:

> *Christ hath redeemed us from the curse of the law, being made a curse for us: for it is written, Cursed is every one that hangeth on a tree: That the blessing of Abraham might come on the Gentiles through Jesus Christ; that we might receive the promise of the Spirit through faith.*
>
> Galatians 3:13-14

We have been redeemed from the curse of the Law and are set in line for blessing. We have already been redeemed; there is nothing more that we need to do. Christ has done it all. With the sacrifice of His life, He purchased our redemption. Our part is to receive His sacrifice and to lay claim to our rights and privileges in the Lord Jesus Christ.

Sin has brought the curse of the Law upon us. There has been a lot of teaching that goes along with this curse. Pastors tell us that God wants us to be sick, poverty-stricken, and shamed. It is amazing how tradition has blinded us to the truth of God's eternal, unchanging Word. We are redeemed, and God is looking for those who will worship Him regardless of their external circumstances.

Even after we become worshipers, it may take some time for us to truly receive all that belongs to us. One of the fastest and easiest ways to receive deliverance from the curse, however, is to worship the Lord from the heart. Say to the Lord, "Lord, I thank You that You have redeemed me from sin, sickness, diseases, poverty, and destruction. I want to worship You and adore You for Your abundant mercy and grace." This type of worship and adoration begins to open the door for us to receive those things that God has for us. Lay claim to God's promises; cleave to them. If you are a born-again child of God, you are a partaker in the New Covenant, and its promises are yours.

God's covenant with us is sealed in the precious blood of the Lamb of God, the Lord Jesus. What a wonderful covenant we have with our God! Our Heavenly Father wants us to receive all of His blessings, but we cannot receive them if we are bound up in sin, tradition, or false teaching.

The promises of the Word of God are not without conditions. God has set certain conditions that we must meet in order to receive from Him. We must prepare ourselves and fulfill our responsibilities if we are to receive all that God has for us. Part of this preparation is the decision that worship will be an integral part of our everyday lives. We must choose to worship. We must also choose not to listen to the unbelievers who try to talk us out of our blessings.

God wants to bless His people in every way He can: spiritually, physically, mentally, and financially. Do you want the blessings of Abraham to rest upon you? You can know this blessing, if you are willing to fight against the forces of evil to receive it.

Is your lifestyle one of worship? Does your heart yearn for those times spent in the presence of the Lord? Do you have a sense of communing with the Lord as you go about your daily activities? As you learn to walk in this spirit of worship, you will come to know the blessing of the Lord more richly in your life. And you will also come to know what I call pro- phetic worship.

WHAT IS PROPHETIC WORSHIP?

And He hath put a new song in my mouth, even praise unto our God: many shall see it, and fear, and shall trust in the Lord.　　Psalm 40:3

Praise ye the Lord. Sing unto the Lord a new song, and His praise in the congregation of saints.
　　　　　　　　　　　　　　　　Psalm 149:1

154

Prophetic Worship

Have you ever become so overwhelmed in the presence of the Lord that you no longer knew what to say or do? Sometimes we are so overcome with His presence that we must simply be still, basking in His presence, loving Him without words.

And sometimes something very wonderful and touching happens: the Spirit begins to give us a new song, a song we have never heard before. How lovely! How meaningful! How precious! When we don't know what to say, God gives us a song that expresses what we wanted to say, but couldn't. Often such a song comes pouring forth like rivers of living water. When the Lord gives a song in the heart, the music and the words fit together beautifully.

One day I was out walking and praying, preparing my heart for a miracle service. I began to worship, and the Lord dropped a song into my heart:

ALPHA AND OMEGA

You are Alpha and Omega,
The Beginning and the End.
You're my Saviour, my Redeemer,
My Deliverer and Friend.
You're the Word of God Incarnate,
You're the Sacrificial Lamb.
You're the Lord of all creation,

My Lord, the great I AM.
Oh, Holy, Holy, Holy, Holy!
You are Holy, oh, Lamb of God!
Holy, Holy, oh, Holy!
You are Holy, oh, Son of God!

© 1993, Daniel D. Rodes

When we sing in the Spirit, whether in tongues or in our native language, we are singing what the Lord places on our hearts. This is beautiful, both to experience and to hear. Paul wrote to the early New Testament believers:

> *Speaking to yourselves in psalms and hymns and spiritual songs, singing and making melody in your heart to the Lord; Giving thanks always for all things unto God and the Father in the name of our Lord Jesus Christ ...* Ephesians 5:19-20

As you become accustomed to worshiping the Lord in this way, psalms, a type of spiritual poetry, may begin to come to you. At times, the words will rhyme, and, at other times, there will be no rhyme at all, but the rhythm will carry the psalm. Regard less of the form, the psalm is a beautiful expression of worship.

How beautiful it is to have the Lord give us songs as we worship Him. Truly, He is a gracious God.

Prophetic Worship

WORSHIP BRINGS THE ANOINTING

And it shall come to pass in that day, that his burden shall be taken away from off thy shoulder, and his yoke from off thy neck, and the yoke shall be destroyed because of the anointing. Isaiah 10:27

Many people seek after the anointing of the Lord, but He does not pour it forth on just anyone who desires to have it. It comes through an intimate relationship with the Lord in which we seek Him daily and spend time honoring Him with our worship.

The anointing He sends upon us is His power that destroys the heavy yokes upon the necks and the burden upon the shoulders of those who are bound. The anointing is important to us as Christians. The word "Christ" means *anointed one,* and we are to be anointed ones as well.

The anointing is a very precious gift that God gives to those whom He can trust. That trust must be earned over a period of time. Although someone may be anointed for a time or may meet the conditions for the anointing at a certain point in his Christian life, if that anointing is not handled in a sacred and reverent manner, it can be lost. If someone wants to carry the anointing so he can boast of it or show it off, he has completely missed its value.

When we enter into true worship the anointing will begin to flow in us, no matter whether we are worshiping at home, at church, or elsewhere. In order to have that anointing upon us every day, there are several things that we should do. First, we must surround ourselves with the Word of God. We should read the Bible every day, meditating upon God's Word and filling ourselves with it so that we can speak it forth. When we quote the Scriptures, we are speaking God's language.

In addition to being surrounded by the Word, we must have a continuous communication with the Lord by praising Him and thanking Him for His goodness, mercy, and love. We must pray continually for the Lord's direction and guidance, worshiping Him from the heart day after day.

Our attitudes and spirit must be right before God. We must continually be aware that the anointing comes from God Himself. It is God who has anointed us by His grace, not because of any accomplishment of our own. We must make certain that all honor and glory goes to Him and not to us. We must be aware that only God's obedient children can be trusted with the anointing. Finally, we must be stable in God, devoted to Him on a daily basis and not having an "on-again, off-again" walk with God.

The anointing is a priceless treasure, given by God's grace, but it can also be very costly. Every person I know of who has been greatly anointed to perform a specific ministry or task has had to pay a high price to receive and keep the anointing. I am not referring to those who claim to have the anointing but are walking in mere emotionalism or in sin; I am referring to those who are dedicated, stable, godly, holy, reliable, dependable people. Such men and women are able to withstand the wiles of the devil, defeat the powers of darkness, and rise in victory every day.

This type of anointing may call for long hours of prayer and much time spent alone with God. It may require arising in the wee hours of the morning to pray, or being called to prayer or worship at inconvenient times. The Lord often tests us to see if we are willing to pay the price for the anointing and the sense of His presence. There is a high cost to the true Pentecost. God can only use vessels that are pure, holy, and clean.

Worship Brings Revelation

And the Lord answered me, and said, Write the vision, and make it plain upon tables, that he may run that readeth it. For the vision is yet for an appointed time, but at the end it shall speak, and not lie: though it tarry, wait for it; because it will surely come, it will not tarry. Habakkuk 2:2-3

Allow your hungry heart to reach out to God. Come to the place where you are lost in a deep spirit of worship — not making a request for anything, but enjoying being alone with the Lord as your heart drinks in the majesty and wonders of His presence. Once you have experienced His presence and felt His love, you will seek His face often. Oh, the joy of seeing the Lord and of hearing His voice!

As you develop a heart of worship, the Lord will begin to speak things to your heart. He may give you thoughts or impressions; He may give you specific words; or He may show you things in visions. You may not receive an open vision, in which you see as clearly as with your natural eyes, but you will be able to see things in the Spirit that the Lord wants to show you. He may show you something to help build your faith or to encourage you. He may show you what is happening in the spiritual realms while you are worshiping Him. He may show you hurting people in the nations of the world and how you can help to reach them. He may show you someone who is in need and how you can help them. Whatever He reveals to you, it will be to bless and encourage.

As you worship, the Lord will reveal Himself to you in ways you have never seen Him before. God loves us so much, and He wants us to live in His presence. Unfortunately, for whatever reason, many believers cannot seem to receive all He has for them. If we come into His presence often, we open ourselves to more knowledge and revelation of His person.

As you seek Him, the Lord will begin to show you how much He cares about you. He may show you something in the future that He wants you to pray about or to prepare for. He will show you how special you are to Him and how much He loves to have you worship Him. Sometimes He may give you a warning about a false teacher or some other danger. He may show you how to minister to someone's need. He may give you a word of knowledge or wisdom that you could never have thought of on your own. I marvel time and time again at the wisdom of God.

Jesus promised us:

> *Howbeit when He, the Spirit of truth, is come, He will guide you into all truth: for He shall not speak of Himself; but whatsoever He shall hear, that shall He speak: and He will show you things to come.* John 16:13

Paul wrote to the church at Corinth:

> *But as it is written, Eye hath not seen, nor ear heard, neither have entered into the heart of man, the things which God hath prepared for them that love Him. But God hath revealed them unto us by his Spirit: for the Spirit searcheth all things, yea, the deep things of God. For what man knoweth the things of a man, save the spirit of*

*man which is in him? even so the things of God
knoweth no man, but the Spirit of God.*

1 Corinthians 2:9-11

As you come into a more intimate relationship
with the Lord, He will begin to reveal to you the
true meaning of His Word. Some Scriptures which
you have found difficult to understand will suddenly become clear as the Holy Spirit reveals their
meaning to you. You will begin to better understand
the heart of God toward His people. The teachings
of Christ will become like a river of life, flowing forth
from you. Even the harsh messages of the prophets
will become precious to you. The whole Bible will
become a field of hidden treasures, and as you dig
deeper, you will find more and more riches.

Worship brings us near to the heart of God where
we may learn those things that *"eye hath not seen,
nor ear heard, neither have entered into the heart of man."*
The Holy Spirit reveals these things to us as we learn
to love the Lord, to obey Him, and to serve Him from
our innermost being. Unless we learn to worship the
Lord and to communicate with Him on a heart-to-
heart level, we never will know all the wonderful
things God has prepared for us right here and now.

The Holy Spirit may remind you of a Scripture
through revelation. He may want you to lay hold of
a particular verse for a time of coming need, or He

may want to remind you of something you need to know. Jesus said:

> *But the Comforter, which is the Holy Ghost, whom the Father will send in My name, He shall teach you all things, and bring all things to your remembrance, whatsoever I have said unto you.*
>
> John 14:26

One day the Lord spoke a portion of scripture into my spirit: "... *nothing shall by any means hurt you*" (Luke 10:19). That statement, though not even an entire verse, became lodged in my mind and heart for several days. I kept repeating, *"Nothing shall by any means hurt [me]."* This happened over a period of so many days that I began to wonder what that meant to me personally. Then, one day something terrible happened. I was holding a small can of gasoline over the carburetor of a bus we were giving to another church when a spark from the engine caught it on fire. When I jerked back my arm, the gasoline flew out all over my clothing and caught fire. Flames leaped from my arm and seemed to be all around me. It all happened so quickly that I later could not remember what I said or did at that critical moment, but almost immediately the fire was snuffed out on my arm and clothing.

I was left a little dazed by the incident, realizing that I could have been very badly injured, yet feeling no pain at all. When Esther later checked my arm to see if I had been hurt, she found that my clothes were not burned and that not even the hair on my arms was singed. A deacon from another church, a man who didn't believe in miracles had been there trying to start the bus and witnessed this event. He later said, "Well, now you know how Shadrach, Meshach and Abednego felt when they came out of the fiery furnace unharmed."

When we make a decision to worship the Lord, God will manifest Himself in our lives and preserve us from impending disasters. When we live in His will and obey Him, He will protect us. Worship helps us to become sensitive to His voice and the warning that He wishes to place in our spirits. And the more we learn to worship Him, the easier it is for us to hear these warning signals.

Worship brings the blessing of the Lord into our lives in so many ways. More than anything else, living a life of worship allows us to know the presence of the Lord on an ongoing basis and to come into a deeper relationship with Him. How wonderful it is to live a life of praise and worship!

— 11 —

THE CONNECTION BETWEEN WORSHIP AND HEALING

Part of our ministry is to conduct healing crusades, and it has been our privilege, therefore, to see the Lord work His miracles of healings by faith for His people. When we are conducting such crusades, one of my primary responsibilities is to make certain that the atmosphere is filled with the presence of the Lord.

There is no set formula by which the Lord's presence may be guaranteed, but we have found worship to foster an atmosphere in which the presence of the Lord is welcomed. We carefully select the praise and worship songs to be used, looking for those that seem to encourage the flowing of the anointing of the Lord.

Then, as the presence of the Lord begins to fill the house, we often experience the wind of the Spirit blowing across the congregation. There have been times when the anointing has been so powerful that people have fallen, slain in the Spirit as this wind blows.

This wind is unlike the natural wind in that it brings us into the very presence of the Lord. When this happens, there is no question of whether we are feeling a draft or a breath of Heaven. The worship and praise that fills the air at such times is indeed precious. Even many people from churches where they have never experienced a manifestation of the power of God in this way begin to worship the Lord.

These things don't happen in every service, but when they do happen, we do our best to respond to the Spirit as He desires to move. It is only when we are prepared and ready, coming in a spirit of expectation, that the Lord visits us in such a manner. It may take some time spent in corporate praise and worship before the Holy Spirit will visit us in such marvelous ways.

We are finding more and more, as the years come and go, that we cannot control the Holy Spirit, nor can we make things happen. We must simply prepare ourselves and let the Holy Spirit do His work. One thing we have found is that the Spirit often comes in waves. There may be a wave of healing for a certain length of time, another wave of the wind, and another wave of the precious glory of God — which often comes in the form of a cloud, shafts of light, or a misty haze over the people.

I believe the day is coming when all of these things will be manifested in most of the true Christian gatherings across the nations of the world. The Lord is visiting His people once again, and we must prepare for the coming glory. But just because it is coming doesn't mean we will all see it. We must be prepared — in righteousness, in holiness, and in worship.

WORSHIP COMES BEFORE HEALING

And, behold, there came a leper and worshipped Him, saying, Lord, if Thou wilt, Thou canst make me clean. And Jesus put forth His hand, and touched him, saying, I will; be thou clean. And immediately his leprosy was cleansed.

Matthew 8:2-3

This leper came to Christ with a great need. Leprosy is a terrible disease, and during that time it carried with it a sentence of ostracism for the afflicted ones. Shunned by society, lepers had to cry out as they went, warning the people, "Unclean! Unclean!" Yet Jesus welcomed the leprous ones.

When this man came to the Lord, I believe that it was His worship that touched Christ's heart. The

Lord Jesus responded as no other would have dared; He reached out His hand to touch the leper. Think about that: Jesus was a healthy man, but He touched the leper. It very well may have been the first such touch this man had known in years. And he was cleansed of his disease.

When we hold our miracle and healing services, it is such a wonderful thing to watch the Holy Spirit moving among people, bringing deliverance and setting captives free. I never cease to be amazed at the miracle-working power of God. After we have spent time in worship, the presence of the Lord is manifest. He often begins to reveal the needs of the people through the supernatural word of knowledge.

At times there have been so many healings and miracles that I have had to dismiss myself from the presence of people and separate myself to a place where I could be alone and weep for joy as I thanked the Lord from the depth of my heart for His work. I am grateful that the Lord uses me to carry on His work on the Earth. When we are vessels fit for the Master's use, He will always receive all honor and glory. It is my sincere desire to spend the rest of my life bringing glory to the precious name of Jesus. How wonderful He is!

There is a song that we often sing during our miracle services. People have testified that they have been healed as they heard this song, because it points to the Lord Jesus as the Healer:

The Connection Between Worship and Healing

LORD, YOU'RE HEALING ME

Lord, You healed the brokenhearted,
You caused the lame to walk.
You healed the sick and dying,
You caused the dumb to talk.
You healed the blind Bartimeus,
Caused his eyes to see.
And Lord, I want to thank You,
For now You're healing me.

Lord, You healed the lame and crippled,
And You made the leper whole.
Lord, You cast out evil spirits
And restored the wounded soul.
Lord, You calmed the stormy tempest
When You sailed on Galilee.
Lord, You calmed my troubled spirit,
And now You're healing me.

Lord, You healed a man with dropsy,
And You raised a widow's son.
And You held those little children,
And You blessed them one by one.
And You healed a paralytic,
And You walked upon the sea.
What a mighty healing, Jesus!
And now You're healing me.

CHORUS:
I thank You, Precious Jesus,
I know You died for me.
I thank You, Holy Jesus,
You died to set me free.
I thank You, Blessed Jesus
For Your death on Calvary.
I thank You, Healing Jesus,
And now You're healing me.

MIRACLES OF THE OIL

It is significant that in our ministry we have several times experienced miracles associated with the oil used in anointing people for healing. Because oil is symbolic of the Holy Spirit, we need the oil of the anointing of the presence of the Lord to flow through us, if we are to be used in the service of the Lord. God has emphasized this to us through the miracles He has given.

During a certain healing service we were conducting, the Lord led me to have an anointing service at the close of the meetings. Up to that time, we were not using oil for anointing the sick and most of the healings were occurring because of the word of knowledge or the laying on of hands.

Since we had not been using oil, I had only a small

bottle that I carried in my pocket, and it was only a quarter full. When the Lord spoke to me about anointing everyone, I looked at that bottle and asked, "Is that all the oil we have?" It was. I thought about sending one of our workers to a nearby store to pick up some more, for surely we would need more than we had. But we got busy, and I forgot to send anyone.

It was only after I had anointed several hundred people that I remembered that there was so little oil. I turned to one of the members of our ministry team and asked, "Where are you getting the oil to anoint all these people?"

"Out of this bottle," he replied.

When I looked at the bottle, it seemed to have about the same amount of oil as it had when we had started. We used that same bottle of oil for several weeks after that, and the Lord kept replenishing it.

What was most amazing to me about that miracle was that I had put some spices in the original bottle of oil and, even though it had been miraculously replenished, the oil we were using in subsequent weeks still had the scent of the original oil. How great is our God!

Since then, this miracle has been repeated on a number of occasions. I have taken a nearly empty bottle of olive oil and, as I poured the oil on the people, the source in the bottle was miraculously multiplied. In fact, after the bottle was completely empty, I would turn it upside down and more oil would run out, and I could anoint more people

Some may consider this to be an unusual miracle, but if the Lord can turn water into wine and fill the widow's vessels with oil, it shouldn't seem strange to us to see Him work such miracles on our behalf in the closing days of the twentieth century.

Another miracle of the oil we have experienced first occurred during a healing crusade. After we had worshiped the Lord for some time, I began to lay my hands on the sick and on those who needed deliverance or some other kind of miracle. As I did so, oil started coming out of my hand. Until that time I had never heard of such a thing, and I didn't know what to make of it. We all began to rejoice in the Lord for such a wonderful miracle. Since that time we have seen it happen on a number of occasions, but every time it is exciting and just as precious as if it were the first time. Later, we learned that others have experienced the same miracle.

We have seen so many wonderful miracles over the years, yet we are still filled with wonder every time the Lord works a miracle among us. I believe that in the future, we will see more and more anointed hands, with the oil flowing from our holy hands to minister to the needs of the people. Our God knows no limits. He wants to work miracles among us. Our part is to come into a position where we can totally depend upon Him for everything, including His miracle-working power. And worship is the key. The more we commune with the Lord in worship, the closer to Him we will grow, and the more fully He will be able to work in us and through us.

— 12 —

WORSHIP AND THE COMING GLORY

Be glad then, ye children of Zion, and rejoice in the Lord your God: for He hath given you the former rain moderately, and He will cause to come down for you the rain, the former rain, and the latter rain in the first month. Joel 2:23

Be patient therefore, brethren, unto the coming of the Lord. Behold, the husbandman waiteth for the precious fruit of the earth, and hath long patience for it, until he receive the early and latter rain.
James 5:7

We are living in a day when we need to prepare for the coming rain — the outpouring of the Holy

Spirit. I believe that the day is coming when *"the early"* and *"latter rain"* will come together, and we will see the greatest revival ever known in the Christian world. We have seen some rain from time to time throughout Church history; but the day is coming quickly when the Earth will be drenched in a downpour of the Spirit of the Lord God. In that day, there will be a mighty outpouring of the Spirit that will exceed anything that has been known thus far. I believe that day is at hand.

Because of this, it is now time for the Church to arise in worship. We must fight like never before in the Spirit, gaining ground for our Lord. It is time for us to arise and become the victorious Church that the Bible declares us to be. It is time for us to declare war on all the powers of darkness. It is time for us to rise up and practice what the Bible teaches about praising, lifting holy hands, dancing, marching, shouting, laughing, and worshiping our God.

The war between good and evil must be fought by victorious, obedient, God-fearing believers. As we lift up the wonderful name of the Lord Jesus and go forth in His mighty power, we will have the opportunity to overthrow the devil and his hordes and to hinder his work. Then we will begin to see the heavens opened and the early and latter rain poured out.

In the Spirit, I have seen droplets of golden rain flowing from the fingers of worshipers and have actually felt the raindrops falling on me and on those who were present with me.

Once we were standing outside of our church building, and the presence of the Lord was unusually strong. Out of a clear and cloudless sky droplets of rain began to fall. We knew that it was not physical rain, but the rain of the Spirit that the Lord was sending upon our church.

It is difficult to comprehend all the wonderful things the Lord is doing in these last days, but isn't it wonderful that we can be part of it? We must intercede and pray for the glory of the Lord to come and for His rain to fall upon us. It is time to lift up the sword of the Spirit and march through this land in triumph. We will be victorious. And very soon we will meet the Lord in the air as we come to the moment of final victory.

WHEN WE HEAR THE TRUMPET BLOWING

When we hear the trumpet blowing
And the saints of God arise,
And the hypocrites are worried,
For it caught them by surprise,
And the sinners shocked and wondering
What has happened to the crowd,
While we give a shout of victory,
Meeting Jesus in the cloud.

Seven Keys to Victory

Brother, don't you dare forget it:
What the Master says, He'll do.
Every promise that is written,
God declares it to be true.
All those scoffers who were mocking
What the Bible has to say
Will be crying, "God, have mercy!"
When it is too late to pray.

Let us keep our eyes on Jesus,
For the day is nigh at hand.
For the signs of His appearing
Show themselves from land to land.
Brother, sister, are you ready
Should this Jesus come today?
Are you ready for His coming
When He takes His Bride away?

There are many gone before us
Who were heroes in the fight.
In the midst of all the chaos,
Kept on fighting for the right.
They considered war their duty,
Fighting every battle well.
They refused to fall in battle
As they fought the powers of Hell.

CHORUS:
Let us set ourselves to battle,
To defeat the evil one.

Worship and the Coming Glory

God declares us to be winners
Through the Blood of His dear Son.
We will never lose in battle
Over Satan, death, and sin.
Through our Captain we will conquer,
And with Jesus we will win!

HOLY SPIRIT POWER FOR PREPARATION

Jesus said to His disciples:

But ye shall receive power, after that the Holy Ghost is come upon you: and ye shall be witnesses unto Me both in Jerusalem, and in all Judaea, and in Samaria, and unto the uttermost part of the earth. Acts 1:8

We can never know the fullness of the power of God in our lives unless we come into a place of worship. Every church and ministry leader must recognize, therefore, the importance of the life of worship, personally and corporately.

In Charismatic circles there has been a great deal of teaching on praise, but what often seems to be lacking is scriptural teaching concerning worship. If you want to see the power of God in operation, and if you want to have miracles happen in service after service, you must learn how to worship God in the Spirit.

The Holy Spirit will move among those who give Him His rightful place. He will operate to the fullest measure only when we offer God the praise due to His name. And little or nothing can be accomplished until the Holy Spirit takes His rightful place in our midst.

Worship Brings the Glory

The presence of the glory of God has been experienced in the past:

> *And Moses was not able to enter into the tent of the congregation, because the cloud abode thereon, and the glory of the Lord filled the tabernacle.*
>
> Exodus 40:35

> *And it came to pass, when the priests were come out of the holy place, that the cloud filled the house of the Lord, So that the priests could not stand to minister because of the cloud: for the glory of the Lord had filled the house of the Lord.*
>
> 1 Kings 8:10-11

God wants to manifest His glory in our midst today, and we must prepare for the coming of great glory. We have seen only a little of what the Lord wants to do. There is coming a day of the full manifestation of the glory of the Lord. As we fast, pray, and intercede before Him, it will come. As we worship the Lord and seek His face, He will show us the changes that we need to make in our lives in order to be ready for that great day of visitation. I often think of Isaiah's experience. He said:

> *In the year that king Uzziah died I saw also the Lord sitting upon a throne, high and lifted up, and His train filled the temple. Above it stood the seraphims: each one had six wings; with twain he covered his face, and with twain he covered his feet, and with twain he did fly. And one cried unto another, and said, Holy, holy, holy, is the Lord of hosts: the whole earth is full of His glory.*
>
> Isaiah 6:1-3

When God's glory is manifest in a great way, we, like Isaiah, will be able to much more clearly see how great, awesome, and holy our God is.

We must welcome the glory. We must look for it. As we wait, we must lay aside our petty differences and focus on the greatness of our Savior and Redeemer. It is not enough for us to be worshiping together with others; our spirits must be attuned to each other. We can achieve this only when each one is attuned to God. This is what happened on the Day of Pentecost:

And when the day of Pentecost was fully come, they were all with one accord in one place. And suddenly there came a sound from heaven as of a rushing mighty wind, and it filled all the house where they were sitting.   Acts 2:1-2

The believers were not just *"in one place"* as they awaited the coming of the Holy Spirit; they were also *"in one accord."* I believe that before long, the glory will be coming to such an extent that *"the whole Earth [will be] full of His glory"* (Isaiah 6:3).

The Lord once showed me a vision of the coming glory. I stood in awe at the splendor and beauty of such a manifestation of the presence of the Lord. He spoke to me and said, "There will be people walking the streets in some cities. As the intercessors are praying, the glory of the Lord will come upon the city, and those people will fall on their faces and cry out to God for mercy." May the Lord hasten that day! And may the Church be prepared and ready to experience the fullness of His glory.

WORSHIP AS INTIMACY WITH GOD

As we worship, we learn to know God more and more. We grow in our love for Him. And, as we begin to catch sight of our God, of who He is and what He is like, we grow to be more like Christ Jesus:

Worship and the Coming Glory

Beloved, now are we the sons of God, and it doth
not yet appear what we shall be: but we know that,
when He shall appear, we shall be like Him; for
we shall see Him as He is.   1 John 3:2

As we worship the Lord, we take on His holiness and His love. We learn what pleases Him and what hinders His power from working in us to its fullest measure. We learn to please the One we love.

It may seem, at first, that you are at a loss for words to express your heart's desire to such a wonderful and loving Lord and Savior. But the more you worship Him, the more you will find the words you need to express your love to Him. As your love for Him grows, you will find yourself saying things to the Lord that you would never have thought of in your natural mind. As you spend more time with Him, you will become more educated to His ways. You will then willingly come under His gentle correction as He forms you into a vessel fit for His use.

When we learn to worship in spirit and in truth, we begin to understand who we are in Christ. We begin to see our place in God's plan for His Kingdom, we are cleansed of pride and false humility, and we gain a truer concept of who we are in the total picture. John the Baptist put it this way:

He must increase, but I must decrease.
                                    John 3:30

Some people seem to think that they can live a haphazard, unconcerned life-style and still maintain intimacy with the Lord. This is impossible! We must live a life of complete surrender and devotion to our heavenly Father before we can enjoy these intense times of worship. There are so many excuses for those who fail to take the time to pray and worship the Lord. God can help us to manage our time so that we can spend more time with Him. If we really desire to read His Word, to pray, and to worship, it is amazing how many of our excuses for not doing so are found to be just that — excuses. There are very few real reasons for not spending time with God.

Paul wrote:

> *For ye are bought with a price: therefore glorify God in your body, and in your spirit, which are God's.* 1 Corinthians 6:20

HOW TO WORSHIP

We are all learning together how to worship God more effectively. I doubt that anyone has yet reached the highest pinnacle of praise and worship, or that anyone fully understands the anointing or how it operates. We must be diligent to continually hear the Holy Spirit as He teaches us. We dare not hesitate or become reluctant to enter into a deeper and more meaningful life of worship.

Worship and the Coming Glory

The Lord is still teaching me, and I believe He will do so as long as I continue to heed Him and to search the Scriptures to understand what I am hearing. Recently, I had a revelation that took me one step closer to understanding the coming glory.

I had been praying over a specific geographic area for some time. There was a lot of evil activity going on there, and I was doing battle with the sins of the place. As I drove past there one day, I noticed a strange cloud that came down and covered the valley. I wondered why it was so foggy there, because it was a beautiful, sunny day. When it didn't seem to be fog, I thought it might be smoke. But as I paused to look more closely, I felt the presence of the Lord and realized that I was seeing the glory of God filling that valley. Praise God! What an encouragement to intercession!

When God shows us visions like this, all we can do is worship Him. I believe we will see more and more of the glory of God in the very near future. We can expect *"the whole earth [to] be filled with the glory of the Lord."* We must continue to teach about the coming glory and to maintain our enthusiasm for praise and worship that will usher in that glory. Let us continue to walk in holiness and righteousness, for that is the only way we will be able to experience the glory of the Lord. And let us continue to grow in biblical truth.

Worship Makes Us More Like Him

Believers who really want to walk with God and to grow in grace are often full of questions: How do I receive the anointing? How do I walk in victory over sin and the enemy? How do I grow in worship and praise?

I have found that the answers all boil down to one thing — obedience. Are we willing to take the Lord at His Word? Are we willing to lay aside the traditions of men and to grasp those things the Bible clearly teaches? I am not speaking here of those obscure passages, not clearly laid out for us in the Bible. These are the matters that so often claim our attention, but God wants us to concentrate on those things that are made clear in His Word.

Draw near to the Lord with a pure heart. Seek the Lord, and walk in obedience. Worship Him in the way He desires, not necessarily in the way you have been taught or are comfortable with. Be willing to lay aside self to gain the privilege of coming into the manifest presence of the Lord.

There is a high price to the anointing. Have you made the decision to pay that price? It may be even higher than you anticipate. Sometimes this can be a lonely road; yet we are never alone. And what price is too high, if we gain intimacy with God?

Worship and the Coming Glory

Come into the presence of the Lord. Rejoice in Him, sing to Him, praise Him. Lift up holy hands before the Lord. March, laugh, shout the shout of victory. Dance before the Lord. Above all, worship Him. Use each of these expressions of worship and praise as the Lord leads; but be sure your worship is in spirit and in truth. And never forget, He is worthy of all of our praises!

Worship Songs

By

Daniel D. Rodes

Alpha and Omega

Words and music by Daniel D. Rodes

You are Al pha and O-me- ga, The Be- gin- ing and the End. You're my Sav- iour, my Re- deem- er, my De- liv- er- er and Friend. You're the Word of God In- car-nate, You're the sac- ri- fi- cial Lamb. You're the Lord of all cre- a- tion, my

Lord, the Great I AM. Oh, Ho- ly, Ho- ly. Ho- ly, Ho- ly. You are Ho- ly, oh Lamb of God. Ho- ly, Ho- ly, oh Ho- ly, You are Ho- ly, oh Son of God.

We Will Dance Before the Lord

Words and music by Daniel D. Rodes

191

Lord, You're Healing Me

Words and music by Daniel D. Rodes

Lord, You healed the brok-en heart-ed. You caused the lame to walk. You healed the sick and dy-ing. You caused the dumb to talk. You healed the Blind Bar-ti-meus, caused his eyes to see. And, Lord, I want to thank You, for now You're heal-ing me.

Chorus I thank You, Prec-ious Je-sus. I know You died for me. I thank You, Ho-ly Je-sus. You died to set me free. I thank You, Bless-ed Je-sus, for Your death on Cal-va-ry. I thank You, Heal-ing Je-sus, and now you're heal-ing me.

When We Hear the Trumpet Blowing

Words and music by Daniel D. Rodes

When we hear the trum- pet blow- ing and the
saints of God a- rise. And the hy- po- crites are wor- ried, for it
caught them by sur- prise. And the sin- ners shocked and won- der- ing what has
hap- pened to the crowd. While we give the shout of vic- tory, meet- ing
Jesus in the cloud.

Chorus

Let us set our- selves to bat- tle to de-
feat the e- vil one. God de- clares us to be win- ners through the
blood of His dear Son. We will nev- er lose in bat- tle o- ver
Sa- tan, death and sin. Through our Cap- tain we will con- quer, and with
Je- sus we will win.

- *Notes* -

Notes –

Ministry address:

Daniel D. Rodes
Truth, Light and Life Ministries Int.
Route1 , Box 108
Mt. Crawford, VA 22841
(540) 234-0225